Mindful Moments for Stressful Days

Mindful Moments
for Stressful Days

Simple Ways to Find Meaning and Joy in Daily Life

Tzivia Gover
Illustrations by Kent Lew

STOREY
BOOKS

Storey Books
North Adams, Massachusetts

The mission of Storey Publishing is to serve our customers by publishing practical information that encourages personal independence in harmony with the environment.

Edited by Deborah Balmuth and Karen Levy
Design and illustrations by Kent Lew
Text production by Kent Lew
Typeset in Cycles, a typeface by Sumner Stone
Indexed by Nan Badgett / word·a·bil·i·ty

"Make a Family Coat of Arms" on page 90 was inspired by Sidney B. Simon's book *Meeting Yourself Halfway: 31 Value Clarification Strategies for Daily Living*, Hadley, MA: Values Press, 1974.

Printed in China by C & C Offset Printing Co., Ltd.
10 9 8 7 6 5 4 3 2 1

Library of Congress Cataloging-in-Publication Data
Gover, Tzivia.
    Mindful moments for stressful days : simple ways to find meaning and joy in daily life /
        Tzivia Gover ; illustrated by Kent Lew.
            p.   cm.
    ISBN 1-58017-428-0 (alk. paper)
    1. Meditation. 2. Attention — Religious aspects. I. Title.
BL624.2 .G68 2002
158.1'2 – dc21   2001049754

For Richard Gover, my father, who says, "Be positive."

ACKNOWLEDGMENTS

Nothing we accomplish is accomplished alone. I want to express my thanks to all of my teachers (those who signed up for the job and those who did not), including the senseis who taught me at Valley Women's Martial Arts and the Northampton Zen Studio; the rabbis and teachers at Congregation B'nai Israel in Northampton, Massachusetts; the late Jane T. Howard; Jane Porter; and My Little Goose, a.k.a. Miranda, who has taught me the great wisdom that only children know. I also extend my gratitude for their help, support, and guidance day to day and moment to moment to Susan Beck, Jane Covell, Jan Freeman, Elise Gibson, James Gover, Molly Hale, Lesléa Newman, Aja Riggs, Diane Steelman, Betty Swain, and Joanne Yoshida. And for filling the moments of my life with love, Chris Swain.

I'd also like to thank the inspirational team at Storey Books, especially Karen Levy and Deborah Balmuth, who helped shape and edit this book.

Table of Contents

Bear in Mind

MANY OF THE WORLD'S RELIGIONS celebrate the blessings of everyday life. The 16th-century saint Teresa of Avila said that she could find God as easily in the kitchen among her pots and pans as she could at the altar. Judaism instructs its followers to offer prayers of thanks for everyday moments, honoring everything from eating a slice of bread to seeing a rainbow, and Buddhist instructional stories often feature an ordinary seeker who finds enlightenment while performing such daily chores as carrying water and chopping wood. Faith traditions around the world agree that, when approached consciously, day-to-day living can be — if not a mystical experience — at least a deeper, richer, and more meaningful one.

Drawing on this rich history, *Mindful Moments for Stressful Days* offers ideas for living a conscious life that fit among the clanging of pots and pans in your kitchen. The tips in this book can help you live purposefully and presently in the moments that you least expect: standing in line at the grocery store, waiting at the airport, working out at the gym. My premise, that living in the moment can deepen your everyday experiences and put you in touch with joy and inner peace, does not challenge any other spiritual practice you may undertake. Rather, this book seeks to enrich the life of the soul and enhance the quality of your days.

The ideas presented here are divided into sections and grouped according to the daily activities in which many of us engage. You can read the book from cover to cover or dip into those sections where you most need inspiration and motivation. Remember: These are suggestions, not instructions. Don't try to incorporate all of these tips and ideas at once. Choose the ones that work for you in the context of your life.

A mindful life is a creative life. Look for opportunities to add your own mindful practices to your daily routine. Celebrate each moment that you can truly say, "I am here."

Roll Call

ON THE FIRST DAY OF FIRST GRADE your teacher called your name and you learned to reply "present" or "here." You answered the question honestly. Not only were you sitting in your seat, but also you really were present. As a child, when you painted, you dipped your whole hand into the jar of finger paints and wiped the colors across the shiny paper. When someone knocked over the castle you built in the blocks area, you cried in protest until your lip quivered. At snack time, the chocolate cookies tasted so splendid with a Dixie cup filled with milk that you dipped one into the other and relished every messy bite.

If someone were to call your name today, right now, could you honestly reply "present"? Have you delighted in the color of a flower, the sky, or another person's eyes today? Did you truly taste the explosion of flavor when you bit into that slice of cherry pie you had last night for dessert? Are you still simmering over a wrong done to you 10 years ago? And right now, as you read this, how much of you is here and how much of you is lost in memory, regret, or nostalgia? Is part of you looking into the future, running down paths of hopes, plans, and dreams?

Living fully in the present moment can seem difficult. After all, *now* is constantly evaporating and reconstituting itself. It may feel like a challenge to keep a toehold on this scrap of time floating past in the ocean of eternity. And why should we take the trouble to pay attention to each moment? Who has the time to stand still, anyway? There is so much to do. There are children to raise, bills to pay, meals to cook, and goals to accomplish.

> *"Seize from every moment its unique novelty and do not prepare your joys."*
> — André Gide, *The Fruits of the Earth*

You can live in the moment and still keep your job, parent your children, reach for your dreams. You can and will do everything you've always done before. You'll still get angry, lose your keys, run out of gas. Being present doesn't solve all your problems, but

2

it does enrich your experiences. It helps you choose your reactions to life's inevitable ups and downs and increases your ability to feel joy and let go of judgment. Living mindfully allows you to make choices from a place of compassion rather than from one of competition, and it trains you to respond with gratitude rather than with greed.

A moment comes and goes in the blink of an eye. To be ready for it takes practice. Let this book be your guide to entering the present moment fully and consciously, with a focus on integrating mindful behavior into your everyday life. Start now. Notice your breath as it enters your nostrils. Observe how it pauses before riding out on your exhalation. Feel your muscles soften. Relax your eyes, your jaw, and your neck. Notice your mind settling gently into stillness.

Welcome. Here you are.

Mind Full, Mind Empty

All of the world's great religions address the idea of mindfulness or contemplative living. In recent decades, in light of the rise of technology, violence, and commercialism in this country, Buddhist teachings on mindfulness have become increasingly popular. Simply put, mindfulness is the state of being fully engaged in the present moment. It is the art of paying loving attention to all that you experience.

But at first glance the term *mindfulness* seems to be a study in contradictions. In any mindfulness practice the first lesson is to empty your mind. So why don't we call it mind-emptiness instead? For one thing, you first need to empty your mind in order to refill it consciously. We meditate to empty our minds. Then we develop the skill of intention to direct our minds positively.

There is a Zen saying, "A cup is useful in its emptiness." In other words, before we can fill a cup with the liquid of our choice, it must be empty. A cup, of course, is also useful in its fullness—

but only if it's filled with what you need and want. In this respect, your mind is no different. Is your mind filled with thoughts and feelings of your own choosing? Or is it cluttered with unexamined responses to past events? Chances are you don't even know half of what is stored in there. And yet the thoughts in your mind rule how you act, how you feel, and how you see the world.

"Nothingness is being, and being is nothingness."

— Daniel C. Matt, *The Essential Kabbalah*

To live mindfully is to be conscious of your thoughts and feelings. It is to live in harmony with your deep inner wisdom and natural state of compassion, forging rich connections to the world around you. To be mindful means to be thoughtful in the truest sense of the word.

Nothing Doing

When was the last time someone praised you for doing nothing? We associate doing nothing with a host of negative judgments, believing it is pure laziness to sit around and be idle. "Stop daydreaming," our teachers and parents often admonished. To simply sit on the porch and pass half the day, as Thoreau reported doing in *Walden,* is considered a waste of time.

Yet there is value in being still. The ancient Greeks thought so. They considered doing nothing the path to wisdom and the highest good. Give yourself permission to do nothing. In fact, give yourself praise. Buy a package of gold star stickers like the ones your teachers used to hand out in school for perfect penmanship. Put one on your calendar or in your planner for every day you take time to do nothing.

Magnify the Good

When you think a thought, you release it into the universe. It gathers energy and returns to you in some way. If you are always sending out complaints and judgments about lack and misery, you'll see these things return to you. In spiritual terms, a thought is a form of prayer: You send your hopes, wishes, and expectations to the force or being you think of as good, generous, and capable of answering your deepest questions.

"The smile that you send out returns to you."

— Indian saying

Psychologists confirm that thoughts have the power to influence experience. The "Expectancy Theory" holds that your thoughts influence your behavior and your behavior tells people how they should treat you. Their behavior in turn confirms your thoughts about yourself and the world. Try sending out positive thoughts. Focus your mind on gratitude; concentrate on appreciating beauty, small gifts, and everyday treasures, such as having food available at breakfast, lunch, and dinner. Such thoughts gather energy and return to you, increasing the love, joy, and peace in your life.

Practice Perfect Acceptance

You don't need anything else to happen in order to be complete. There is nothing to fear and nothing to want in this moment. Accept this moment as it is. Sure, there is plenty that is wrong, unjust, and unfair in the world. You can practice perfect acceptance and still take action against wrongdoing; you can work to improve unfair systems whether they are at home or in the world at large. The challenges are on the path, but you step into them one perfect moment at a time.

Inbreath

Respiration, inspiration, spirit. Notice that all three words have a common root. That's because they are all related. In Genesis, God kisses life into Adam; God breathes existence into his creation. With a gulp of air and an exhaled stream of sound, each of us is born. It's stunningly simple: One breath is all that keeps us on this narrow path between living and dying. Breath is our most basic connection to life; it unites mind and body. Breathing is also our connection to spirit, to soul.

The profound, life-changing practice of meditation may simply consist of sitting on a chair or cushion and paying attention to your breath. What could be easier? But in practice, one breath, two breaths, maybe three, and then most people find themselves thinking about something—anything—else. But it's worth the effort. Paying attention to your breath can improve your health, your level of alertness, and your ability to live in the present moment.

Live and Learn

Your breath has a lot to teach you. Each time you exhale you let go, trusting intuitively that there will be another inhalation to keep you alive. Yet we spend so much of our time grasping, holding on for dear life to things that aren't nearly as essential to our physical survival. We hold on to hurtful ideas and hurtful relationships. We even hold on to good things, clutching so tightly we nearly choke the life out of them. Today, listen to your breath and heed its message. It is saying, "Let go, there is plenty more."

> *"Breath is life, the basic and most fundamental expression of our life."*
> — Sogyal Rinpoche, *The Tibetan Book of Living and Dying*

Don't Hold Your Breath

Many Eastern religions believe that the lower abdomen is the seat of vital energy and power. But how often do you let your breath reach deep into your belly instead of stopping it in your chest? How does your breathing change when you face difficult emotions?

Notice what is happening around you when your breathing becomes shallow or when you hold your breath. Ask yourself

9

why you are stopping the flow of air. Remember, when you stop breathing you are cutting off your connection to the present moment. Next time you are in a stressful situation, take a few deep, cleansing breaths. Become aware of how this simple act can change how you feel and how you respond.

Give and Receive

When you breathe you create a connection to the world around you. You take in molecules from your environment, absorb them

into your body, and integrate them into your physical being. When you exhale, you release molecules that have lived inside you. As you breathe, you take what you need from the world and use it for your own survival, then release the air that trees and plants need for theirs. With each moment you give and take. Notice how you give and take in other areas of your life. Are you hanging onto possessions you no longer need? Find something in your home that you no longer need and give it to someone who may find it useful.

Quieting the Monkey Mind

Meditation teachers often talk about "monkey mind," a habit of undisciplined thinking. Scientists have identified the limbic system, an older, more primitive region of the brain, as being associated with impulse and emotion. Unchecked, our minds are ruled by primitive desires. We grab at what we believe we need for survival. Impulses dominate and pull us into self-pity and rage. Anger leads our thoughts on a wild ride through feelings of revenge and resentment. Attraction may lead us into relationships that are inappropriate.

This barrel of monkeys in the mind can send us in circles controlled by ambition, fear, lust, and confusion. Meditation is the discipline that helps put our wisest self back in charge. It returns the mind to a clear, uncluttered state. With meditation we can move past confusion and reconnect with the true mind that the 17th-century philosopher John Locke called "that eternal, infinite Mind, who made and governs all things."

Meditation does not necessarily mean sitting on a straw mat or cushion with your legs pretzeled into lotus position while chanting foreign syllables—although it can mean just that.

"At any rate, that is happiness; to be dissolved into something complete and great."

— Willa Cather, *My Antonia*

Meditation can also mean sitting up in your favorite chair with your eyes closed, paying attention to your thoughts. There are many ways to meditate, and detailed instructions can be found in countless books and classes on the subject. For now, just learn a few basic meditation techniques and begin to practice them. The act of meditating, in whatever form you choose, may be your most valuable tool in learning to live in the present moment.

You Are Here

In the Old Testament, each time God called to a prophet and a prophet called to God, they were answered with the words "Here I am." They didn't say, "I'll be there in a minute, after I balance my checkbook and pick up my daughter from softball practice." They didn't say, "Let me check my hair and makeup and I'll be right with you." No, they were present when the call came.

Living in the moment gives you the ability to answer fully and honestly, "I am here to fulfill my purpose." Try using the phrase "I am here" as a focal point when you meditate.

Open Your Eyes

Meditating is about being fully awake and alive. Try meditating with your eyes open—you will have less chance of falling asleep or drifting into an unconscious, dreamlike state. Direct your eyes at a 45-degree angle toward the floor. Keep your focus relaxed;

don't stare intently at a single object. Allow your gaze to fall on the empty air midway between your eyes and the floor. This will take some getting used to, but once you adjust you may notice you can focus your mind more easily with your eyes open.

Where One Thought Begins

When you meditate, try to observe the point where one thought ends and the next begins. You will start to see your thoughts as though they are beads on a necklace. Now try to notice the space between thoughts. Become aware of this space increasing. Don't force it to expand, just observe. The more you practice seeing the interval between thoughts, the more that empty space will naturally elongate.

"Both in and out of the game and watching and wondering at it."
— Walt Whitman, *Song of Myself*

Listen for the Quietest Sound

Meditation is deep listening. Find a time and place to sit quietly for a few minutes. Try to listen for the quietest sound you can hear. At first it may be the laundry tumbling in the dryer. Keep listening. Can you hear the flow of electricity through the wires? Keep listening. Can you hear your heartbeat? Let your ears be open and relaxed. Keep listening.

Meditation off the Mat

It is good to meditate just to meditate, and it is good to focus on your breath just for the sake of focusing on your breath. But unless you want to be present only when you are doing meditation exercises, you will limit the effectiveness this practice can have. It would be like getting physically fit by lifting weights at the gym but then refusing to haul sacks of groceries out of the car with your new muscles. Your hard-won strength would be useless.

Take your meditation practice off the cushion and into the world at large. Apply what you learn in silence to your daily life. Be still and observe your thoughts before you answer the criticism your boss just leveled at you. Do you feel anger rising? Notice the sensations in your body that accompany anger, name the feelings that you experience, but don't let these emotions rule your behavior. Detach from the emotion before you take action.

While on the cushion did you feel a sense of completeness, as though everything in the world was good? Recall that feeling as you approach the customer service desk at the department store to complain about the expensive clock you recently bought that is already three hours slow. Take a breath and explain the situation with a loving, patient heart.

Slow and Steady

Try to spend some time every day meditating. If it's hard for you to sit still for 5 minutes, try it for 4. If you can manage it for 20 minutes, try it for 25. Build up slowly. Practice the art of detaching from your thoughts. We are so used to letting our thoughts rule us that it will take practice to let them go. But this is essential to reclaiming your mind and your life. Building your capacity to meditate helps strengthen your ability to practice the principles of meditation in your daily life.

Watch, Don't Judge

Meditation is about observing in a detached but loving manner. Watch your thoughts, but don't judge them. Don't think, "That's a bad thought" or "That's a good thought." Don't think, "I'm doing this right" or "This meditation is going nowhere." Simply be an observer. If a thought emerges about what you need to do tomorrow, notice *planning;* let the thought pass and return to your observation post. If you start to ruminate on an argument you had with your spouse earlier in the day, just observe *thinking* and let the thoughts pass. If you feel yourself enjoying the sensation of meditating, let that pass, too. Don't hold on. Don't grasp at any sensation, pleasant or painful. Observe and be open.

Now try this technique when you're not meditating. Observe your thoughts when something makes you want to dance, when something makes you want to cry. Notice how your emotions start as thoughts. You can observe them and then let them pass.

Empty Yourself of Yourself

Strip away the layers in which you have wrapped your identity. Move past the resume, the hairstyle, the fears, the failures, the history of hopes and achievements. Let go of your likes and dislikes. Now ask, "Who is there?" Keep digging until you hit something that is glowing. Something that is eternal. That's your self. That's where meditation will take you. It will be there whether you "succeed" or "fail." It is always yours and always you.

Coming Home

Home. It's much more than just an address. We say home is where the heart is, and there's a great deal of wisdom in that. You might add that home is where the *opened* heart is. Meditation teachers often speak of the importance of bringing the mind home, and philosophers throughout the ages have identified the mind as home to the soul and spirit, in much the same way that the house we inhabit is home to the body. In childhood games we were safe when we reached home base. Ideally, home is the place where when we enter, we feel we belong, and we are safe.

In the physical sense, our home has much to teach us. It is a structure made of stone and mortar or Sheetrock and wood, nails and shingles. We equip our homes with doors, locks, and even sophisticated security systems to keep intruders at bay. Our house is built to keep the rain and cold at a safe distance so we can be warm and productive inside.

We put a lot of attention into choosing our home and how it should look and feel. We consider whether a particular house is near a good school for our children. We may fall in love with a home because of the view of the mountains from the living room, the inviting feel of the wraparound porch, or the apartment building's art deco lobby. We carefully select the furniture we bring inside, visiting several stores before we choose the perfect table. We discard the battered couch we've been dragging from apartment to apartment since college and keep bouquets of daffodils from the farmers' market in the blue glass vase on the kitchen windowsill.

"Only in a hut built for the moment can one live without fear."

— Kamo No Chomei,
12th-century Japanese poet

This is the kind of attention we should pay to our mind—the home we carry with us wherever we go. By paying careful attention, we can outfit our minds to keep our psyches safe, just

20

as windows, doors, and the roof keep us physically safe and comfortable. We can post sentries at the mind's gate to keep out destructive influences and let in helpful ones.

There are many simple ways to redecorate, discard what no longer suits us, shop around for what does, and make ourselves feel more at home, physically and psychically. We can learn ways to be mindful at home, and to be at home in our minds. Household chores and routines that feel like drudgery can offer opportunities to come home to the present moment. And the daily rituals of waking, eating, and going to sleep—practiced with mindfulness— can become more meaningful.

Many Entryways

By the time they enter school, children can recite their address. Adults can usually reel off the street number of every house they've ever inhabited. We are so attached to our physical surroundings that moving is ranked among the top stress-producing events in our lives. But our inner home never changes. We don't need an address to locate it. Like a turtle's shell, this is the dwelling place we carry with us and never outgrow. There is no key to this house, but there are many entryways. Meditation is one way in. Opening your senses is another.

These two concepts of home are related. Just as love transforms the utilitarian bricks and mortar of a house and makes it into home, so conscious living transforms generic minutes into fully realized moments. These moments have a vast architecture of their own; they are places in which you can live, love, and dream.

By paying attention to your physical home, you also nurture your ability to feel truly at home in your psyche.

Locate Your Inner Home

Sit in quiet meditation. When your mind is still and relaxed, open your inner eye and explore. Allow your meditating mind to travel down deep inside you. Look for a calm, quiet place. This place is the seat of your wisdom and intuition. It is the doorway to something we sense as infinite, where we connect with the power some call spirit, God, or simply good. Looking through your mind's eye, describe this place. Are you at the shore of an inner lake? Have you come upon a fountain? A patch of jewel-blue sky? A clean, clear sound? Did you open the door to a dream room where you feel instantly comfortable and at home?

This place exists whether you find it now or whether it takes many attempts to get there. It may be buried beneath fears and anxieties, but it is there. Explore until you find it. Get to know this place by visiting it in your meditations. Come here whenever you need to. This is where you can find peace. Take a drink here, breathe in, and be rejuvenated.

Home Improvement

For today, allow yourself to experience home as a metaphor for the resting place of mind. Each time you think about your house, such as how you'd like to decorate it or where you wish it were located, consider your inner home just as deeply. Make sure you prioritize home improvement projects for your home in both senses of the word.

Come to Your Senses

The five senses are your windows to the world. Think about it. If you didn't have eyes, ears, a nose, nerve endings in your skin, and a tongue, how would you know what existed in the world around you? Your eyes bring you the yellow-green of new leaves, the soft pink inside a seashell, and the majestic profile of skyscrapers. The eyes let you see where you are going and who else is around you. They show you the world's beauty and inspire you to create more. Your ears bring you music, birdsong, traffic sounds, and the voice of a friend asking for help. Ears are the gateway to compassion; they let you know where you are needed. Your sense of smell makes certain foods, and people, seem irresistible. When you smell something, you actually transport atoms of that object into your body. Your sense of smell brings the world inside you and keeps you from remaining separate. Hundreds of thousands of delicate sensory nerve endings in your skin allow you to feel caressed by an embrace, delighted by the feel of water licking your ankles as you wade into the surf, or tickled by an evening breeze. Our ability to touch and be touched starts with the skin. Taste is a magical sense. How do you even begin to describe the taste of a berry, a drop of milk, a bite of rhubarb? Your senses are openings into a mindful life. Make eating a pear a meditation. Light incense or meditate outside on a spring day and focus only on the scents around you.

Add Spice to Your Surroundings

Make sure all of your senses feel at home in your house. Buy a special set of silk or high-quality cotton sheets that are a delight to your skin. Keep a bowl of fresh fruit on your table to add natural hues and aromas to your surroundings. Which pictures, colors, or arrangements of objects are pleasing to your eye? Remove or replace any that no longer please you. Is there a leaking faucet that you haven't fixed and that is setting your ears on edge? Take the steps to repair it. Invest in a white-noise machine or use a fan to neutralize unpleasant noises you can't eliminate. Shop in an ethnic market and notice the variety of scents, textures, and colors. Buy a new vegetable or spice and bring it home to taste and add to your cooking.

Your Front Door

Gateways and doorways have been imbued with special meaning throughout the centuries and around the world. In Japan, the red Torii gates at the entrances to Shinto shrines are striking for their bold and simple beauty. When people pass through these gates, it is said they become purified in heart and mind. Front doors are

"A threshold is a sacred thing."

— Porphyrus, third-century poet

also passageways between the private sphere of our homes and the public realm of commerce and politics. In Jewish homes, a small cylindrical or rectangular box called a mezuzah is fastened to the doorpost. Inside is a scroll with a prayer that includes a reminder to keep thoughts of holiness foremost in one's heart and mind.

26

Take a moment to look at the doorway through which you enter and leave your home. Is there something you could place on or near your doorpost as a conscious reminder of what you want to leave outside and what you want to invite inside? It may be a wind chime whose peaceful music soothes you and reminds you that your home is a place of harmony, or a wreath that symbolizes the life-renewing energies you want to foster inside. Any carefully chosen decoration

that embodies peacefulness and tranquility can help focus your mind on your intention to create a home filled with love and to bring that nurturing with you when you go out into the world. Each time you enter your home, take a breath and renew your commitment to cross the threshold in a peaceful state.

Taming Technology

These days, doorways aren't the only portals into our homes. The television, telephone, beeper, fax machine, and computer all have the potential to be helpful tools or unwanted annoyances that intrude on our mindful state at home. Find a balance for staying in touch with useful technology. For instance, when you log on to the Internet, you open yourself to advertisements, "instant messages," and e-mail solicitations. What do you want to let in and how much of your mind's energy do you want to devote to this electronic portal? Set aside specific times of day to retrieve and answer e-mails. You can also look into features that block e-mails from unknown senders. Consider disabling the "instant message" function if you prefer to maintain a single focus while you are on-line.

Television has the same potential for usefulness or damaging distraction. It lets in not only amusing stories and interesting bits of news but also disturbing images. Even seemingly harmless commercials or music videos may carry messages or imagery that don't support your values and beliefs. Use your VCR to tape and consciously choose what to watch.

Choose Your News

Probably the most difficult time to be fully present is when we experience something unpleasant. Our initial reaction is to detach from what we are experiencing because it is too painful. Yet each day we watch, listen to, or read the news and are exposed to horrifying stories of natural disasters, war, famine, crime, and other catastrophes. If we allowed ourselves to be truly present during the evening news, for example, we might need to watch it with a box of tissues within arm's reach because every story of human suffering would elicit our deepest sympathy. Or we might pack our bags and take the next flight to a war-torn nation to help feed the hungry and heal the wounded. It is impossible to really take it all in.

"Stand porter at the door of thought. Admitting only such conclusions as you wish realized in bodily results, you will control yourself harmoniously."

— Mary Baker Eddy, *Science and Health*

One way to process the news mindfully is to absorb it in small doses, perhaps just a half-hour a day. You may want to take occasional "news fasts" for a day, weekend, or week. You can also choose a news source that is less sensational, such as a morning newspaper rather than an evening television broadcast. If something disturbs you deeply, rather than tune it out, try to commit to a realistic action. Make a donation to the Red Cross to help people who've lost their homes to an earthquake. If a report about global warming produces anxiety, vow to ride your bike to work one day a week instead of taking your car.

Turn Off the Ringer

You are settling in to watch a movie with your family or are about to get into the tub—and the telephone rings. As though that bell were a command to action, you leap up and race to answer the call. Any harmony that had been created in your home, any focus you had managed to establish, is now shattered. You may have left an important conversation with your teenager to answer a call from a stranger trying to sell you a magazine subscription that you don't want. Try setting aside time each day to be "phone-free." Turn off the ringer and turn down the volume on your answering machine. Take advantage of technological offerings, such as Caller ID, which lets you see who's calling before you answer the phone.

Clearing the Clutter

Feng shui is an intricate Chinese system for arranging furniture and other objects in a way that increases positive energy flow and attracts creativity and prosperity. It involves energies attributed to each compass direction, the Chinese zodiac, and a pendulum. But even a novice, equipped with a few basic concepts, can use the feng shui principles to clear clutter in the home and in the mind.

While feng shui is new to many people living in the Western part of the world, just about anyone can attest to the way a simple housecleaning can have positive effects on one's state of mind. Who hasn't experienced a sense of mental uplift after a rigorous spring cleaning, or a renewed perspective after hauling trash bags filled with old clothes and books to the local Salvation Army, or a greater feeling of ease after rearranging the furniture to make a room feel more comfortable? You don't have to buy a compass, acquire a pendulum, or learn astrology to feel the benefits that can come from reconfiguring your physical—and mental—space.

Choose a Room

A good place to start your practice of feng shui is the bedroom, because it is where you sleep, dream, and make love. Stand in the middle of the room. Take several deep, relaxing breaths. Close your eyes and feel your feet planted solidly on the floor. Relax your knees and let each vertebra in your spine rest lightly, one on top of the other. Now slowly open your eyes and walk around the room, maintaining an open and conscious attitude. Notice how you feel as you stand in each part of the room. Does the corner where you keep your bureau feel constricted? Does the bed suddenly feel as though it is in the wrong place? Consider making some changes. Even as small a gesture as replacing an old poster with something new and vibrant, such as a colorful tapestry, can have a positive impact.

Consider Each Object and Each Thought

When you practice feng shui in your home, consider each object and ask yourself, "Do I know this object to be useful? Do I think it to be beautiful?" If the answer to both questions is no, give the object away or throw it out. You can do this with your thoughts as well. In fact, feng shui was originally a mental, not a physical, practice. Sit quietly and examine what's inside your mind. You'll likely find a jumble of worries, thoughts, plans, hopes, and dreams. Pick up each thought one at a time and examine it. Here's an old resentment about the time your best friend forgot your birthday. It's not serving any useful purpose and it's certainly not beautiful, so let it go. That memory of lying on the warm sand and listening to ocean waves during last summer's trip to the seashore? Polish it up and keep it on hand for moments when you want to center your thoughts and relax.

Designate a No-Thoughts Zone

Choose a cozy corner of your home, a favorite chair, or even the shower, and make it your quiet haven. Whenever you come to this spot, agree not to look backward or forward in time. Don't worry and don't plan. Don't follow any thoughts at all. Simply be in the moment. And then in the next.

Everyday Enlightenment

Stories about Zen meditation are filled with accounts of monks attaining deep insights while chopping wood and carrying water. After reading enough of these stories you may suspect that to reach enlightenment you must forgo indoor plumbing and cen-

tral heating in exchange for more modest arrangements. Stories of enlightenment from modern-day seekers demand a more contemporary setting. Chopping wood and carrying water instead may become folding laundry and sorting recyclables. The point, of course, is not whether you are carrying buckets of water or car-pooling children. It's that even the most mundane task, done with a conscious mind, can offer moments of peace, inspiration, and joy.

Follow Your Hands

When performing household chores, try focusing all of your attention on your hands. While pulling laundry from the washing machine, feel the tension in your fingers as you tug sweatpants, shirts, and shorts free from one another. Feel the cold weight of the sheets as you lift them into the dryer. Notice the sensation of the cool metal dial under your fingertips. If any other thought comes into your mind, such as plans for the day or worries about money or your children, let it go and refocus your attention on your hands.

Lavender Therapy

Queen Victoria is credited with discovering that lavender is a tonic for the nerves. Today, aromatherapists agree that lavender can help relieve stress and relax the mind. You can use this scent to make household chores more soothing. Look for lavender-scented laundry products, or simply add a few drops of lavender water to your wash. Notice the scent when you fold clothes, make your bed, or wipe your hands on a dish towel. You can also keep lavender hand cream in your purse or glove compartment and rub some on your skin when you need to calm down. You'll benefit not only from the scent but also from the soothing massage.

Take Out the Trash

When you bring the trash to the curb, meditate on the value of throwing out what you no longer need and want. Just as easily, be willing to leave behind beliefs and patterns of thought that no longer work for you. Imagine old resentments or negative messages about yourself and the world piled into barrels that are then carted away and properly discarded.

Vacuum Cleaner

An empty mind is like a vacuum. Just as your Hoover upright will suck up anything in its path — forgotten coins, paper clips, dust, dirt, marbles — so too will your mind take in anything in its path. In short, unless you're careful, you may wind up replacing one set of harmful beliefs with another. What do you want to use your mind-space for? Make a list of your core values. Every day for 10 days write down the five things that mean the most to you in the world. What kind of a person do you want to be? What is most important to you? Your list may contain anything from dinnertime with your family to the quality of patience to the ecological health of the planet.

When the 10-day period is over, look at your lists. Is something repeated again and again? Is the list consistent or constantly shifting? Find what is common to all of your lists. Write down these values and post them someplace where you are likely to come across them often, such as on the mirror of your medicine cabinet, on the first page of your journal, inside your date book, or on the "to do" list in your electronic organizer. Let these beliefs be in the forefront of your mind, and measure new ideas and behaviors against them.

Wash Your Brain

Brainwashing conjures up images of extreme, cultlike behavior. But brainwashing happens to everyone to a greater or lesser extent. How often have you heard a song on the radio and found the tune running through your mind for the rest of the day? The brain replays the tapes we hear. The tapes playing in your mind today are probably running messages from your childhood. What were you told about yourself as a child? That you were too serious? Funny? Clumsy? Smart? How many of these judgments are still looping through your mind? Have they come to define your self-image? Once you do a thorough inventory of the messages that have gotten stuck in your head, you may choose to keep some and erase others. Best of all, you can choose new tapes to play.

Repeat Your Beliefs

When you meditate or sit quietly, notice the thoughts about who you are that come up again and again. Later, make a list of what you find. If you've been brainwashed to believe you were selfish, consider replacing this old insult with an affirming truth, such as "I love myself and extend that love to all I encounter." If you were told that you are lazy, find a new thought to program into your brain instead. Try something like this: "I enjoy the fullness of time. I rest and relax to energize myself for the tasks ahead."

Whatever you choose as your new affirmation, repeat it over and over again. Remember, you had to hear the negative messages for many years for them to be embedded in your mind. Repeat your new messages 10 times in a row at least 3 times a day. Keep this up for as long as it takes, until you believe the new messages and your actions reflect that belief.

Choose a Mantra

Mantra is a Sanskrit word that means mental protection. Mantras are often given by a guru to disciples, who then repeat them during daily meditations. You can give yourself a mantra, or a word that helps you protect your mental state, and repeat it during meditation or whenever your mind begins to wander to unproductive thoughts throughout the day. One of the best-known mantras is the Sanskrit word for the divine: the syllable *Om*. In English the word *home* sounds very similar, and it can be a good mantra to bring your thoughts back to your center, or your internal home. Any word or phrase that helps focus your attention will work. Try "peace," "I am here," or simply "I am."

Keep Your Place

You can keep your place, literally and mentally, with a simple homemade bookmark. Write an affirmation or a reminder on a sticky note. You may want to write one word, such as *breathe,* or an inspirational phrase or saying, such as this quote from Elisabeth Kübler-Ross: "Learn to get in touch with the silence within yourself and know that everything has a purpose." Write the word or phrase in your best script using a calligraphy marker or a glitter pen. Make it beautiful. Position the paper with the sticky edge at the bottom, so that the clean edge is visible above the page when you close the book. Use this note to keep your place in a journal, daily organizer, book, or magazine. Each time you open it, you also find your place mentally, reminding your-self of where you want your mind to be.

Home Is Where the Hearth Is

You may have an idyllic image of how a family meal should be prepared. Perhaps you picture a pretty woman in a clean apron stirring pots of steaming food for her family. The kitchen is bright and tidy. There are no oil splatters on the stove; there are no sounds of microwaves whirring, children bickering, or phones ringing.

Your experience of cooking may be so far from this ideal that you barely recognize your kitchen rituals as being in the same category. Maybe you grab a microwave dinner from the freezer drawer or rip open a box of pasta and reach for a jar of prepared sauce. You may even pick up sandwiches from the delicatessen on your way home. Once you sit down to a meal, you may worry about what you eat or how much and whether your food is healthful or harmful. Perhaps you harbor fears about whether there will always be enough food or whether you are eating more than your fair share.

Food is a source of strength, but it can also be a source of stress. Our appetites can be confusing, and our reactions to them counterproductive. Taking a mindful approach at mealtime can help address all of these concerns and enhance your experience of eating.

Set the Table, Set the Mood

We talk about setting the mood for an evening meal with fine china, candles, and flowers. But the mood for mealtime goes beyond just the physical niceties. Take a moment to set the mental mood as you prepare dinner. Observe but don't judge the thoughts that are going through your mind as you get dinner on the table. Are you comparing yourself to someone? Favorably or unfavorably? Are you silently grumbling because you feel you are doing more than your fair share of the work? Take a moment to turn those thoughts around and focus on your true intention: to nourish yourself and those you love.

Grocery List

Each week you make a list of what you need to fill your pantry. Make a weekly grocery list for your inner self as well. What do you need this week to continue to nurture your conscious lifestyle? A morning set aside to garden? An hour alone? A long, hot bath? Fresh flowers in your bedroom? A massage? A visit to your spiritual home, be it a church, synagogue, or natural spot that inspires awe in you? Make a "shopping" list of the things you love, the things your heart and soul need.

One Bite at a Time

There is a Buddhist saying, "When I eat, I eat." For those of us who eat while we drive, work at our desks, or read the newspaper, this can be a radical concept. Practice eating a meal without any distractions. Focus only on the scents, tastes, textures, and nutritive qualities of the food you consume. Even if it's uncomfortable—especially if it's uncomfortable—watch what feelings come up. Breathe and take another bite.

43

Just Say Thanks

Focus your mind on the meal ahead by saying a simple thank you. Throughout history and around the globe, people have had to struggle to survive. The quest for food has been an all-consuming endeavor for humankind in most historical periods and places. Meditate on how fortunate you are to have food to eat in every season. Appreciate the fact that you rarely hear your stomach grumble, let alone feel real pangs of hunger. This is an everyday miracle of our time and place, a fact that is all too easy to overlook. Before you take a bite, take a breath. Inhale your gratitude for having your most basic needs met. Exhale any tensions or worries that may interfere with your enjoyment of this gift, and offer a wish that one day all people may be so blessed.

All Join Hands

Focus your attention on the people with whom you share your meal by taking a moment before you eat to join hands. Gently squeeze the hand of the person sitting to your right. As you squeeze, feel your love and appreciation for that person. That

person accepts the gesture by truly receiving the loving intent, and then in the same manner squeezes the hand of the person sitting to his or her right. Continue until the circle is complete. Then release hands and begin your meal.

Mealtime Meditation

Contemplate the food on the plate before you and name every force—human, environmental, and mechanical—that contributed to bringing this meal to your plate. Mentally give thanks to each one. For example, you may give thanks to your spouse for

45

chopping the cucumbers in the salad, your son for washing the lettuce, your daughter for unpacking the groceries, the retired school teacher who bagged your purchases at the supermarket, the boy who rang up your order, the people who stocked the grocery shelves ... and keep going. You'll end up thanking the farm workers who harvested the plants, the rain that fed the seeds, and the sunshine without whose light nothing would have sprouted. Don't forget the truckers who drove the boxes of pasta across the country. Now, with renewed appreciation for your own place in the global web, savor each bite.

Chew Your Drink and Drink Your Food

Take your time with the food and drink you consume. Take a sip of juice and hold it in your mouth until you feel the tastes and sensations of warm and cold melding. When you take a bite of food, chew it thoroughly, trying to identify each flavor, spice, and texture. Not only does slowing down the process of chewing and swallowing heighten your appreciation of what you are eating, but it also improves your digestion.

Kitchen Colors

The kitchen is the heart of your home. It is where you and your loved ones create the nourishing foods that sustain you. Make sure your kitchen contains colors and objects that feed your senses. Hang a framed photograph of your children playing in the leaves, post a quote that inspires your imagination on the refrigerator door, or consider painting the cabinets sunset pink.

Take Time to Smell the Roast

Cooking is a sense-ual experience. Engage your senses of hearing, sight, smell, touch, and taste as you prepare food. Listen to the knife on the chopping block as you slice colorful vegetables, such as red and yellow peppers, carrots, and eggplant, for your salad or stir-fry. Open at least three bottles of spices and sniff each one before you decide which to use. Get your hands dirty. Knead dough or make tuna or meat patties. (Remember how much you used to love making mud pies? This is even better because you can eat the results!) You'll feel nourished before you even take a bite.

In the Garden

Kneel between rows of newly sprouting carrots and beets and begin to work. Pull up weeds and watch what happens inside you. Thoughts seem to quiet down as your attention naturally focuses on the task at hand. Digging in the dirt, planting a seed, adding compost to a flower bed, pruning a shrub — all of these activities seem to absorb you so fully that any other problem or concern is temporarily suspended. Any gardener can tell you that this happens, but it is difficult to say why.

Perhaps engaging with the earth in this intimate way reconnects us with the source of our life and therefore genuinely

48

calms us. It may be that in the garden the elements of earth, air, water, and fire (in the form of light) come into natural balance. The garden is also where growth, the exuberance of life, and the natural process of decay so vividly take place. We are reminded that everything is connected as we haul barrowfuls of plant stems, trimmed leaves, and uprooted stalks to the compost pile and later dig in the newly made soil containing last season's withered plants. In the garden we can be rooted where we are: in the sunshine, in the soil, in the present moment.

Garden Indoors

If you don't have space to plant even a small herb garden, or if it's winter and you can't garden outdoors, bring a plant inside. Clean an avocado pit and suspend it in a jar of water using toothpicks. Place it on your windowsill and watch it sprout roots and shoots. Start an amaryllis

"Cultivate your garden."

— Voltaire, *Candide*

or a paperwhite bulb in winter. Let yourself be absorbed by the plant's slow and confident growth. Breathe in the lessons green things teach us about the cycles of seasons, life and death, and the unity of the elements.

Be Neighborly with Nature

Visit the trees and gardens around your house. Walk through the woods. Learn to name the flowers and plants that grow close to your home. Visit a public garden. Take a moment to sit and reflect on the seemingly endless varieties of plants, the bounty of nature's palette. Inhale and let your mind fill with thoughts of abundance and plenty. Exhale and let go of any fears of stagnation or limitation that you may be holding on to.

Just Add Water

Water has much to teach us about meditation. Water flows, it never fights. It is flexible yet persistent enough to wear down rocks and carve out continents. The sound of water gently falling is as soothing as a lullaby. Consider adding a small fountain or reflecting pool to your garden.

"Yes, as everyone knows, meditation and water are wedded forever."

— Herman Melville, *Moby Dick*

Sleeping and Waking

Mindfulness teachers often talk about the "awakened state." They are referring to something beyond merely opening your eyes in the morning; rather, they are describing a state of aliveness that requires conscious participation. In this state you truly experience reality as it presents itself moment to moment, as opposed to living in an unconscious state with your mind clouded by worries, plans, and unbridled emotions.

Night also offers opportunities for living consciously. When the moon and stars take over the sky, it is a natural time for reflection and turning inward. Take this chance to review the day and, without judging, notice how you spent your time. Did your thoughts and actions reflect your values and best intentions?

By taking time at the beginning and end of each day to come fully into the present, you create a solid framework for your mindfulness practice. You will come to find that, rather than sleeping through your days, you live life with your eyes truly open.

First Thoughts

Let your first meditation of the day take place before you get out of bed. Start by noticing the words and feelings that run through your mind when you wake up. Did your internal chatter wake up with you? Are you already writing grocery lists, planning meetings, and rehearsing speeches before your feet even touch the floor? Are you grateful for the opportunity to experience another day, or are you silently grumbling about having slept too little?

Take a moment to thank the universe for the night of safety that just passed and for having a warm, dry place to sleep. Take three conscious breaths before you take any other action. Focus only on the air entering and leaving your body. If a thought enters your mind, start again.

Don't Be Alarmed

The jolting buzz of an alarm clock truly makes for a rude awakening. Consider purchasing a radio-alarm clock and set it to a station that plays soothing music. Or shop around for a clock that uses chimes or an agreeable tone to help you wake more gently.

You may also want to write an affirmation or a reminder to wake with gratitude on a sticky note and attach it to your bedside clock.

Let There Be Light

Waking up involves making a transition from dark to light. Whenever possible, make this transition a gradual one. Don't turn on lights right away unless you need to. Taking a shower in the mute light of morning, before turning on the electric lights, can be especially soothing. Try lighting a candle in the morning to welcome the light back into your life.

Write from the Start

Start the day with 10 minutes of free writing. This type of writing is as much about listening to your inner voice as it is about composing meaningful sentences. Once you put your pen to paper don't stop—just keep writing. Think of these pages as a river that carries your worries, plans, old patterns, and inner chatter far, far away to a vast and distant ocean. Just write and release. Don't judge or analyze. Don't even reread what you've written for at least two weeks. Remember, this is a meditative practice, not a literary one!

Ten Wonderful Things

Before you go to sleep make a list of 10 wonderful things about the day that just passed. Don't look for only big-ticket items, such as promotions at work, long-awaited achievements, or financial windfalls. While these are exciting and noteworthy, this is a time to reflect on what truly have been moments of wonder. These are your "alive" moments, moments that sparkle. The majestic blue sky you noticed as you were leaving the office. The way your son's freckles seemed to dance across his nose and down his cheeks when he laughed at the story you told. The scent of pine as you walked to the mailbox.

You can make a mental list as you lie in bed waiting for sleep, or you can record your lists in a notebook. You can even compose lists aloud with your family, letting each member share his or her 10 wonderful things before you all wish each other goodnight.

You may find that as this habit takes hold, you notice more and more wonderful moments as you go through your days.

The Moment Sleep Comes

Watch your thoughts as you lie in bed preparing for sleep. See if you can be present enough to notice the moment you cross the bridge from waking to sleeping. (But don't be discouraged if you can't. This is a practice whose reward is in the effort; the goal is rarely met—even by meditation masters!)

A Good Night's Sleep

Getting enough sleep is important to a mindful life. Sleep deprivation reduces brain activity and general alertness. People who are sleep deprived don't properly process glucose, which provides important fuel for brain functioning. To be truly awake, you must first get a good night's sleep.

Dream On

When we drift off into dreams, we enter another area of consciousness—one we shouldn't ignore. After all, we spend one-third of our lives asleep and some fifty thousand hours dreaming. Research shows that the sleeping brain is as active as the waking brain, perhaps even more so.

While not everyone agrees on where dreams come from or what their purpose is, dreams have provided wisdom and guidance to countless generations. From the days of the ancient Greeks, who believed dreams were sent by the gods, to the 20th-century writings of Freud, who purported that dreams arise from repressed desires, dreams have

56

taken hold of the human imagination. Psychologists today believe that dreaming is one way we regulate our emotional lives. When we dream, we process events that we don't get to study in waking life. We review who we are and how we feel about ourselves.

"The house protects the dreamer, the house allows one to dream in peace."

— Gaston Bachelard, *The Poetics of Space*

As you become more conscious in your daily life, your dreams will come into clearer focus, and what once seemed like surreal stories with no apparent meaning may begin to speak directly to your experiences. At times they may offer thought-provoking insights.

To glean meaning from your dreams, you must first remember them. Although the average adult goes through three to four nightly REM cycles, or periods of Rapid Eye Movement, when dream activity occurs, many say they never dream or can't remember their dreams. Recalling your dreams can sometimes feel like trying to catch fish in the ocean with your bare hands. One wrong move and they swim beneath the surface and beyond your grasp. But everyone has dreams, and with a little effort, anyone can recall them.

57

Keep a Dream Book

Archeologists have found evidence that as early as the fifth or sixth millennium B.C., ancient Assyrians kept "dream books." Inscribed on clay tablets were descriptions of dreams that sound surprisingly contemporary: dreams of death, losing hair or teeth, or being naked in public. Keep your own dream journal by recording your dreams in a notebook each morning. Your unconscious mind has been active during the night, and the stories and images it offers up may help you gain perspective on problems or questions that arise during the day. If all you can remember is a single image or an emotion, start there. You may know you dreamed about your mother, but not what happened. Just record what you remember. You can also write a question in your dream book before going to sleep, and then see if any answers arise in the dreams you wake with. Be patient. It may take several nights to sense a clear response.

Make a Dream Pillow

Whether you want to improve your ability to recall your dreams or to enhance the intensity of the dreams you have, a dream pillow can help. It's easy to make your own. Start with a small piece of fabric (the pillow need be only the size of your hand). Choose a material that is soft and durable, such as thick cotton, corduroy, or flannel. Collect some scraps of cloth or cotton for stuffing. Then consult an herbal reference to select some herbs. Different herbs are credited with possessing various dream powers. For example, mugwort and lavender are said to bring calming dreams. You may also want to choose herbs whose scents appeal to you, such as jasmine and lilac.

Cut the fabric into the shape of a rectangle, a crescent moon, or, if you are feeling ambitious, a star. Add a handful of dried herbs and the scraps of cloth to soften and fill out your pillow, and then sew it up. Slip your creation between your pillow and pillowcase. You may find that the very act of creating the pillow focuses your intention to listen to your dreams, and that intention alone can elicit more colorful, creative, and conscious dreams.

Of Sound Mind and Body

As FAR BACK AS THE 4TH CENTURY B.C., when Aristotle posited that the mind exists independently of the body, the two entities have been pitted against each other. The split between the physical and the mental deepened in the 17th century, when Descartes declared, "I think, therefore I am." The neck has served as a boundary, dividing mind from body, ever since.

Scientists and philosophers now challenge this dualistic approach. Metaphysical thinkers, including Deepak Chopra, have helped popularize the science behind the mind's interrelationship with the body, offering a more holistic perspective on our lives and health. Studies have shown that emotional stress can contribute to immunological and endocrinological disorders.

Scientists have also proven that our beliefs about physical pain can influence bodily sensations and that such qualities as optimism, spontaneity, mental efficiency, and happiness can positively impact physical health and longevity.

At the same time, physical exercise has been shown to alleviate depression and anxiety and may even help nerve cells in the brain grow, make better connections, and suffer less damage with aging. As a result of these findings, major hospitals now incorporate meditation and relaxation techniques into their treatments for everything from cancer to chronic pain. It has become nearly as common for a physician to recommend exercise as to prescribe medication. With so much evidence of the link between mind and body, it seems only natural to include physical activities in a mindfulness practice as well as to take a mindful approach to movement.

"To keep the body in good health is a duty.... Otherwise we shall not be able to keep our mind strong and clear."

— Buddha

Build Your Soul's Muscles

These days, most of us know something about what it means to keep physically fit. We measure our blood pressure and watch our weight to assess how well we are doing at keeping our bodies in shape. We wouldn't dream of ignoring what we eat and how much we exercise and expect to be able to run a marathon, or even climb a couple of flights of stairs without getting winded. But we  do just that when it comes to maintaining a healthy mind and soul. We have guidelines for physical fitness, but we have few principles for keeping mentally and spiritually healthy. Even those who attend church or synagogue often forget about the welfare of their spirit and mind during the rest of the week. Yet there are exercises that, with regular practice, can build your capacity to feel joy, contentment, and gratitude. You can build your sense of well-being just as surely as you can build better biceps.

Move Your Mood

If only brooding over a problem were as productive as a hen's "brooding" over her eggs. More often, this type of moody contemplation causes us to stagnate. Rather than meditating productively on a problem, we are suffocated by it. The antidote may be as simple as getting up and moving. Imagine a storm cloud hanging over an otherwise clear sky. Now picture a wind blowing that heavy weather away. Physical movement can have a similar effect on a bad mood. The next time you find yourself brooding over a problem, put on your favorite music and dance around the living room. Or pick up a rake and attack that blanket of fall leaves on your lawn. Watch as your internal storm blows over.

Choose Your Face

There is an expression that says, "Your parents created your face for the first thirty years, you create your face for the next thirty." It means that we inherit our appearance from our parents and grandparents, but we are also responsible for the face we show the world. The thoughts you think each day can add a sparkle to your eyes or pull the corners of your smile down. If you repeat a thought often enough it becomes a belief. A long-held belief can imprint itself on your body as a wrinkle, an upright posture, or a defeated slump. Take a good look at yourself in the mirror. What beliefs can you read in your face and body? Which thoughts about yourself and your life is it time to change?

Mirror Image

Too often we drag our bodies around like so much extra weight. We focus on what we don't like about our appearance. Rather than accept our looks, we judge them. Yet our bodies are part of who we are. If we don't love our bodies, how can we really love ourselves? Next time you look in a mirror, notice what you are thinking. Is it positive or negative? Look yourself in the eye and say something you want to believe about yourself. Tell yourself you are beautiful. How does it feel? Most likely it seems awkward at first. Try again. Tell yourself something positive every time you see your reflection. Look into your eyes and give yourself a compliment. Say, "My beauty glows from the inside out." Keep repeating it. Soon enough, you'll come to believe it. Better yet, it will become true.

Learn from the Pros

Any athlete knows what it takes to get out and jog even if the temperature is plunging outside. A fitness buff knows that the little choices she makes every day add up to physical fitness: ordering a baked potato rather than French fries at a restaurant, parking at the far end of the lot and walking the extra steps to get to the store, or choosing a bike ride with friends over a movie. A conscious mental life demands the same attention to everyday choices. Every minute of every day you can practice the principles of positive thinking, choose love over fear, and attend to the needs of your soul.

Practice, Practice, Practice

How does a professional tennis player achieve success? He doesn't just go out on the court on the day of a big tournament and hit the ball. He practices daily. He breaks down each move of his game, isolating it and then repeating it again and again until he can perform it in his sleep. For example, he may repeatedly toss the tennis ball in the air to perfect the height and speed he wants to achieve for his serve. Next he might swing the racket up over his head and slice down through the air again and again before reintroducing the ball into the equation. When he puts these movements together they have been imbued with a new grace, efficiency, and strength.

To live mindfully you must break your thought patterns down and rebuild them in much the same manner. You start by meditating with no other distractions in order to perfect the art of conscious thinking and breathing. After daily practice, you may observe yourself detaching from an angry thought forming in your head during an argument with your child as easily as you did while sitting quietly on your cushion during meditation practice. After months of repeating an affirmation that reminds you to be patient, loving, and kind, you may notice that when an irate customer confronts you at work, you instinctively respond with a calm attitude and a clear head. Just as an athlete trains to improve her muscles and aerobic capacity, you can train to improve your mental capacity for harmonious and conscious thought.

Imagine Success

Olympic athletes spend almost as much time training their minds for competition as they do training their bodies. Visualization, mental imagery, and "practicing" routines in their minds before they perform are ways they train their brain to respond appropriately when they begin to move. Studies show that visualizing physical events in this kind of detail creates brain activity similar to that which occurs during the actual performance. Too often, however, we rehearse failure in our minds instead. Imagine yourself flourishing at any given task. Visualize the scene of your successful performance in as much sensory detail as possible.

Stretch Your Mind

A runner stretches her muscles to prepare her legs to take longer strides. Similarly, the practice of meditating helps stretch your mind. When you meditate, you expand your mental capacities, elongating the space between thoughts and focusing on the moment when one thought ends and the next begins. As a result, you reach deeper states of consciousness. You can also broaden your mind by considering other points of view. Read a book on a topic you haven't explored before. See a movie that challenges you to think more deeply.

Build Your Heart's Strength

Aerobic activity builds your heart's capacity to pump blood to the rest of your body. Building a strong cardiovascular system also helps sharpen your mind by increasing blood flow to your brain. On another level, you can use aerobic workouts to strengthen your spiritual heart's capacity for compassion, love, and kindness. When you leave the gym, look for ways to exercise your kindness muscles by helping others. Help someone carry her packages. Let the other guy take the first cab that comes—even if you staked out the corner first.

Form Counts

Form counts in sports. It counts with consciousness, too. Good physical posture helps create a clearer mind by opening your breath's passageways and improving circulation. When you slouch, your rib cage caves in, cutting off the flow of oxygen to your brain and making you feel tired. Improved posture can also impact how others see you and how you see yourself. Practices such as qigong and yoga combine breathing techniques with postural alignments to support healing and transformation.

Start with a simple shoulder roll to help you stand and sit a little taller. Sit with your chest open, your neck relaxed and long, and your shoulders pulled back and down. Now roll your shoulders to the front, up to your ears, and to the back so they are down and your shoulder blades pull slightly toward one another. Repeat this shoulder roll several times, ending with your shoulders back and down. This leaves your chest open and relaxed. Now check your mental posture. Are you upholding the values you wish to emulate or are you slouching into negative thinking?

Present (Not) Tense

When you are in tune with your body, you are one step closer to being in the present moment. Take the time to check in with yourself and see how you are feeling from the soles of your feet to your scalp. You can do this almost anywhere—while sitting at work, lying in bed, or driving a car. Starting with your feet, bring your attention to each part of your body. Tense both feet, then slowly let go into full relaxation. Move up slowly, doing the same with your ankles, calves, knees, thighs, lower belly, and so on. Keep breathing as you take note of any discomfort or tension. As you inhale, imagine that your breath is reaching inside to massage any aches or pains. Exhale and release tension. Feel your thoughts settle and your stress dissolve as you enter the present moment.

Take Your Pulse

Enter any fitness center and you'll notice that from time to time people pause and place two fingers on their wrist or neck to check their pulse. It's a good practice. Likewise, you need to stop and take your soul's pulse. Choose a sound or signal that you hear at random intervals throughout the day. If you work on a computer, you may get an audible or visual prompt when mail arrives in your electronic mailbox. Each time you see or hear it, take a deep breath and observe your thoughts and feelings. Notice whether you are relaxed, open, and at peace. Let go of any tensions or worries as you exhale. When you inhale again, affirm that good flows to you from all directions.

Integrated Exercise

Since the early 1960s, Eastern exercise systems, such as yoga, tai chi, karate, and qigong, have been gaining popularity in the West. Part of their appeal may be that these pursuits exercise more than just the body; they also integrate spiritual principles and conscious breathing. You can explore these physical arts or simply adopt some of the principles of mind-body unity into your own physical fitness routine. Use your workout time to address your source—however you define it. Ask the big questions and listen for answers.

Balance Your Workout

Tai chi is a system of exercise that seeks to balance the principles of yin and yang. Simply put, yin and yang are complementary principles found in nature: soft and hard, male and female, hot and cold. When properly balanced, these seeming opposites flow together to create a sense of unity and wholeness. Whatever form of physical fitness you engage in, notice whether it addresses the wholeness of your being. If you only lift weights, consider adding a softer activity, such as swimming, to your regimen. If a lunchtime racquetball game is your primary source of fitness, try alternating your games with a more peaceful yoga class or a stretching routine.

Train Your Mind While You Train Your Muscles

Instead of reading a magazine or watching television while you're on the treadmill, use the time to meditate and reflect. One way to meditate is to let your mind wander freely through any thoughts and feelings that bubble to the surface. Observe your thoughts without judging them. Notice what you are thinking, but don't try to direct your mind.

Another option is to use your workout time to focus your mind on an inspirational phrase or value that you'd like to bring into a situation with which you may be struggling. For example, if you are having difficulty in a personal relationship, you may want to meditate on the meaning of forgiveness. Visualize your emotional heart expanding as your physical heart becomes stronger.

Yoga Means Union

Yoga derives its name from a Sanskrit word that means union with the divine. Hatha yoga, the branch of yoga consisting of physical postures, or *asanas*, has become the most popular form

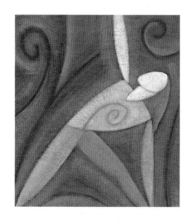

in Western countries. Other forms of yoga focus on serving the divine spirit and seeking transcendental knowledge. Modern research has shown that yoga, a five-thousand-year-old practice, can heighten relaxation, improve concentration, and reduce chemicals in the brain that cause anxiety.

Vital to any yoga practice is conscious breathing. Whether or not you take yoga classes, you can attain some of yoga's benefits by learning the basics of yogic breathing. Practice by making your exhalation slightly longer than your inhalation. Try this whenever you feel stress or just need to center your mind and body. Whatever form of exercise you pursue, try to make your breathing a more conscious part of the activity.

74

Celebrate Your Body

Too often we take our bodies for granted. And when we do pay attention to our physical selves it is often for the purpose of "improving" our bodies by working out, dieting, or grooming. Take some time to truly appreciate your body. Look for excuses to sensually enjoy and indulge yourself. If you're going to the gym, pack a scented body splash in your bag and use it to refresh yourself after a workout. Leave time for a sauna or steam bath after an exercise routine. Whether you are lifting weights or running to catch a bus, enjoy the feel of your limbs moving. Feel yourself settle into your thighs, your belly, your skin.

The Other Endorphin High

Author Harold Kushner says doing good for others is the spiritual equivalent of an endorphin high. You can make your physical fitness routine reinforce your overall effort to live a more conscious life by giving your workouts a higher purpose. Sign up for a walk-a-thon or road race to raise money for a charity you care about. Get a spiritual endorphin high along with the real thing.

Walk the Walk

Ever notice how from Biblical days to contemporary times, prophets and sages are always walking long distances? Moses trekked through the desert, Tibetan Buddhists walk and chant, and Gandhi walked for peace. Putting one foot in front of the other seems to have a spiritual dimension. Certainly there is evidence that walking soothes the mind.

One reason walking may nurture a sense of wholeness is that the opposing motion of the right arm and the left leg swinging forward together, then the left arm and the right leg doing the same on the alternating stride, exercises both sides of the brain in a harmonious rhythm. But whatever the physiological explanation, incorporating purposeful walking into your life can increase your ability to feel peaceful and centered. You can achieve the benefits of walking whether you stroll down country roads, stride through city streets, or pace in place on a treadmill.

On Your Feet

When you are walking, whether it's from your car to your front door or from your home into town, don't think about only getting to your destination. Instead, think of each stride you take as a complete action in and of itself. *"Not all those who wander are lost."*

— J.R.R. Tolkien, *Lord of the Rings*

Make each step a full, rocking motion. Place your heel on the ground and feel each inch of your foot as it meets the earth. Feel yourself finish the step as you push off from the ball of your foot and begin the next stride.

Step into Happiness

There is a point on the bottom of the foot that acupuncturists call "Bubbling Spring." Pressing on this point, which can be found just below the ball of the foot in the center of the sole, is thought to help alleviate depression. When you walk, you naturally massage this point with every step. Take a 20- to 30-minute walk and feel your mood lighten and lift.

Learn a Poem As You Roam

Choose an inspirational poem or a prayer and commit it to memory while you walk. (Poems that rhyme or have a clear structure are the easiest to memorize.) A good way to do this is to write the first several lines or the first stanza on a sticky note, the next group of lines on another note, and so on. Place these notes one directly on top of the other and stick them to your water bottle. As you jog, walk, or work the treadmill or stair machine, silently repeat the lines on the first note until you can recite them without looking. Peel off that sticky note and start on the next part of the text. Soon you will have a library of inspirational literature in your mind. Now you can meditate on any of these poems or prayers whenever you please.

One Word at a Time

Another good way to meditate while moving is to focus your mind on a poem or prayer one word at a time. Say a word silently to yourself and let your mind run over associations with the word. Let the layers of meaning resonate through you like the full sound of a bell. Move slowly from word to word. You can easily pass 20 minutes or a half-hour on the treadmill, in the pool, or on your jogging route using this mental exercise. When you are done you will feel a deep sense of calm, as the wisdom of your chosen passage sinks into your being in a new way.

Dream Routine

A morning walk is the ideal time to meditate on a dream you had the night before. Replay the dream in your mind. Pay attention to the feelings that come up as you scroll through it. Analyze the dream as if everyone in the dream were a part of you. What could your subconscious be trying to tell you?

Meal Plan

We don't need scientists to tell us that the food we eat can affect our mood, but studies are re-inforcing the merit of this commonsense wisdom. Notice how you feel after a breakfast of pancakes, sausage, and homefries. For the rest of the morning you may feel sluggish, as though a haze has descended on your mind. That's because high-carbohydrate foods increase your brain's supply of the amino acid tryptophan, which is like nature's sleeping pill. Also, heavy foods, especially fats, are difficult for the body to process, so digesting them saps your energy. If instead you eat a breakfast of fruit salad with a small serving of yogurt and even a scrambled egg, you will feel lighter and your mind will be clearer and better able to focus. High-protein, low-carbohydrate meals help boost your mental power and keep you alert. When choosing what to eat, consider the time

80

of day and the task at hand. Selecting foods in this way can make your mind, as well as your body, feel fit.

Eat and Be Merry

When you are deciding what to eat during the day, choose proteins; they increase levels of the amino acid tyrosine, which the body uses to make energizing brain chemicals. Raisins, apples, and nuts, which are rich in the chemical boron, are thought to boost attention and memory. Some foods even boost your mood. Omega-3 fatty acids, which are present in salmon, tuna, sardines, flaxseed oil, and walnut oil, may help fight depression and increase brain function. Foods high in carbohydrates are good for an evening meal. They help your mind relax and get ready for sleep.

How much you eat can also affect your mind's ability to function at its best. According to the National Institute of Aging, a diet of 1,800 to 2,000 calories per day, depending on your body size, is best for optimum brain functioning. When calorie intake is kept at about this level, brain cells increase their production of certain proteins, which in turn help neurons function at their best.

Drink to Your Mind

The brain is composed of about 90 percent water—a higher percentage than any other organ in your body. Water carries oxygen to all your cells, including those in your brain. Just as athletes are encouraged to drink plenty of water before, during, and after a big game, those who want to improve their mental performance will benefit from doing the same. Keep a bottle of spring water in your car, by your bed, and at your workstation. Sip often.

Other beverages can affect your mental state as well. A glass of warm milk with a dash of nutmeg can help calm your mind. Peppermint tea can help you unwind. Peppermint relaxes muscles —and when it comes to relaxing, the mind often follows the body's lead. If you want to feel more alert, a cup of green tea, which contains a small amount of caffeine, can help.

Food for Thought

Everyone knows what physical hunger feels like: distinct pangs and sensations that clearly indicate the body needs food. There are noticeable signals when you have neglected the nourishment of your mindful state as well. Trouble falling asleep, being easily provoked to anger, and feeling lonely are signs of spiritual hunger. Notice your feelings. They may be signals that you need to feed a different kind of hunger.

Proper Diet

A good diet consists of the proper amounts of vitamins and minerals. To keep mentally and spiritually fit, be sure to get your Recommended Daily Allowance of inspiration. Stock your bedside table with books of poetry or stories of people who have battled great odds to achieve great good. Read a few pages before you go to sleep and before you get out of bed in the morning. Seek out someone to talk to whose life inspires you to live up to your ideals.

Fasting with Food

Many spiritual practices require followers to fast from food. In Taoism, disciples are asked to fast instead from thoughts, concepts, and words in order to clear and refresh their minds. Meditation is one form of fasting from thoughts. You can also set aside a day to fast from complaining or any other negative habit of mind.

The Ones
You're With

THERE'S AN OLD BUDDHIST STORY about a man who climbs a distant mountaintop to study with a wise monk. After years of meditation practice he seems to have reached enlightenment, so he sets off to return to his village. Soon he passes the home of a peasant woman who is washing her clothes. She empties her washtub and accidentally splashes him with dirty water. The man loses his temper. He must return to the mountaintop. Years later, the man feels he has finally reached enlightenment. Again, as he heads back to his village, he passes the house where the woman is doing her laundry. Again he is splashed with dirty water. He loses his temper and once more must return to his meditation practice.

As difficult as the years of solitude and study were for this seeker, facing the mundane realities of life among everyday people was even harder. This is a common challenge. The present moment can seem like a difficult enough place to reach just by itself. You put all of your resources into getting there. You meditate, you breathe, you practice. Finally, you find yourself in the Promised Land of loving acceptance. You've decided to watch anger pass like a dark storm cloud and not grab hold and take a ride on it. Then you return home to find that your partner has left a sink full of dirty dishes, or your daughter refuses to get out of bed and the school bus is on its way. You feel your frustration rise. Your serene mood disappears.

"Let me not look for what I can get, but for what I can give. Let me not seek so much to be loved as to love, to be consoled as to console."

— St. Francis of Assisi

Now we understand why monks seek solitude. It is the easiest way, perhaps the only way, to maintain perfect peace. But the fact is that we share this planet with more than six billion other people. Interacting with others, whether they share our goal of living a mindful life or not, can be the most difficult—and the most important—work we do.

Staying Connected

An important part of keeping in tune spiritually is acknowledging the broader context of our lives. There are many ways to do this. One simple way is to sit quietly and focus your thoughts on this moment and nothing else, just the time it takes to breathe in and out. Now think about the past hour and all that happened in it. Broaden your internal vision to the day that just passed, then the week, the month, and the year. Reflect briefly on your life to date. How long has it been? Thirty years? Forty? Fifty? There have been countless minutes, hours, weeks, months, and years along the way, and each one seemed very important at the time.

Think about your parents and grandparents. Holding three generations in your mind, it's hard to fathom all the moments that were lived by all those people. But keep going. Your grandparents had parents, too. And so did they. Let your mind go back as far as you can, generation by generation. So many people with whom you are connected have lived and died, struggled, succeeded, and failed in various ways. Entire civilizations, in fact, have come and gone.

Now go back to your breath. In and out. Look ahead. Perhaps you have children. If so, imagine the children they will have or do have. If you don't have children of your own, picture the children

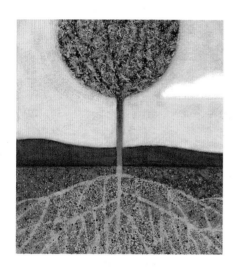

you know. Then picture them growing up and having more children, and those children having children, and so on. Again, come back to your breath. Acknowledge the importance of your life, the sacredness of it, but also try to hold the vision of yourself as one link in a chain that stretches backward and forward into infinity.

Every minute counts. Every decision we make affects generations. And yet, three generations from now, the details of this lifetime will be forgotten. This mixture of valid self-importance and true humility represents a paradox worth embracing. Each life is but a moment in the flow of eternity. Yet this moment of being connected to the generations that came before and those yet to come is the most important moment of all.

Take a Family History

Using a large sheet of newsprint and colorful markers, make a family tree. In addition to simple genealogy, use this tree to chart the history of beliefs into which you were born. Under each relative's name write a quote or saying that sums up his or her philosophy on life. Grandma Fanny's quote may be the phrase she repeated each Sunday as she kissed you goodbye after your weekly visit. Perhaps she always said, "Be the best you can be." Uncle Fred may never have said much, but he had a kindly, though defeated, demeanor. His silent message may have been, "Good guys finish last."

Fill in as many relatives and their "quotes" as you can. Now look it over and see what beliefs you've inherited. Is there a relative you can look to when you need inspiration? Has there been a strong pull in your family toward fearful and negative messages about life? You may find beliefs you'd like to let go of. Picture

Uncle Fred in your mind and tell him that it's okay to be a good guy. Watch him stand taller; feel yourself do the same. As you do this exercise, you may identify helpful beliefs and negative thought patterns that have been unconsciously handed down to you. You may also unearth some spiritual role models in your own family.

Make a Family Coat of Arms

In addition to wearing full armor, medieval knights donned a coat of arms when they charged into battle. This highly decorated symbol included a crest and motto, symbols and sayings that reminded knights of their purpose. Make a coat of arms with your family to affirm the values and beliefs you hold dear. This exercise involves thoughtful discussion as well as creativity, so be prepared to work on it over time.

Start by drawing the shape of a shield on a large piece of paper or oak-tag. Divide the shield into sections by drawing one line down the center, then two lines across the top and bottom. You now have six sections to fill. In the first one, draw a picture that represents a value your family cherishes, such as a lion to symbolize strength or a bird to embody freedom. In another section, draw a series of pictures that represents the individual strengths of each family member: a laughing mask for the member who provides humor, a spoon and fork for the one who nourishes others with food, and so on. Use another section to represent a common value to which your family aspires. It may be community involvement, spiritual growth, or family togetherness. Other blocks can be used to illustrate your family's ancestral roots and dreams for future generations.

Reserve the last block for the family motto. This can be a sentence or just several words that sum up your collective goals and values — "Unity, Caring, and Compassion," for example. Be as creative as you like. Once you design your family coat of arms, use it as a pattern for a rug or quilt, make a carefully painted version to frame and display in a prominent spot, or copy it into a family album.

Do unto Others

A mindfulness practice seems naturally to produce a feeling of connection with all people and all beings. Our innate springs of compassion bubble to the surface. To make compassionate action a part of your mindfulness practice, set up a "Do unto Others" calendar. Post reminders to yourself to volunteer, donate money to charity, write a letter to the editor, or help a neighbor. Encourage your friends or family members to join in.

Community Development

People throw the word community around as though there is a preexisting group of like-minded people who support and nourish one another, and all you have to do is find it. In most cases, however, you have to create it. Consider starting a group of your own. It doesn't need to have anything to do with mindful living on the face of it. Any time a group of people comes together over a period of time there is the potential for helping, caring about, and supporting one another. Start or join a parenting group, book group, men's or women's group, community chorus, knitting circle, or cooking club. Put up a notice in a library or community center to form a meditation or study group. Use this opportunity to create community in your life — consciously.

Listen Up

There's one mindfulness skill that can improve your relationships with others, and you can practice it nearly every minute of every day. In fact, you do it all the time, naturally. Now try to do it consciously: Listen. Hearing and listening are not necessarily the same thing. Studies show that immediately after hearing someone talk, most people remember only half of what was said. In addition to being an essential tool for effective communication, good listening can help ease stress and improve relationships.

Start listening right now. You may hear a distant siren, the wind blowing outside, the whirring of a computer, or the rumblings of your refrigerator. You may hear the sounds of lives being lived around you: doors closing, squirrels scurrying, the neighbor's dog protesting his solitude. When you listen more deeply you can hear things in the stillness. Listening with your ears, with your heart, and with your entire being is a way of being receptive. When you truly listen you will feel porous, open, and relaxed.

Your Authentic Voice

There is a way to always know whether what you are hearing is your authentic voice or the babbling of your ego. If the voice is urging you to be peaceful, to take positive action, it is your authentic self. If it is complaining, wanting more, or wishing ill on anyone or anything, that's your ego. Ask it to please keep the noise down. Tell it to take a number—you'll get back to it later.

"God's one and only voice is silence."
— Herman Melville

The Art of Listening

Put on a tape or CD and make yourself comfortable on the sofa. Do nothing but listen. If your mind wanders to a thought, gently lead it back to the music. Hear each note without anticipating the next. It may help to focus on a single instrument. Imagine you are riding the music the way a surfer rides the waves, rising and falling in perfect balance as the melody carries you. Other ways to practice the art of listening include learning to play an instrument, learning birdcalls, or taking up a new language.

Easy Listening

So often our environment is cluttered with noise: a television left on that no one is watching, music piped into stores, blaring advertisements, people talking on cell phones or arguing next door or at the next table. Tune into the sounds around you. Are there unappealing sounds you can eliminate? Switch on a fan to neutralize those you can't turn down but want to screen out. Select soothing music (harp music and piano music can be particularly relaxing) as a pleasant sound background.

Quiet Your Inner Chatter

Sometimes we don't hear another person speaking because we're too busy listening to the chatter inside our minds. We're wondering how we look, planning what we're going to say next, or judging what the other person has just said. All of this adds up to the equivalent of inner white noise. Make eye contact with the person you are speaking with. Mute the television, turn off the radio, and settle into a receptive posture. Uncross your arms and lean slightly toward the person speaking. Touching her arm or shoulder while she speaks can also help focus your attention on what she is saying.

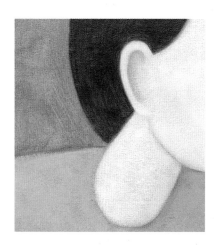

Take Turns

Practice the art of listening with people you are close to, such as a partner, mature child, or friend. Here is a good exercise to do if you are working through a problem together, especially one you've been having difficulty resolving. One person takes a turn speaking. The other person listens without interrupting. The speaker has a set amount of time, up to three minutes. If possible, use an egg timer or another device to keep time and announce the close of the period with a bell or tone. Otherwise, the listener can keep time using a watch. The listener's job is to hear what the speaker says without making judgments or forming a retort in his or her head. (Don't be surprised if this is difficult to do.)

When the speaker is finished, the listener tells the speaker what he or she heard. The listener does not offer commentary, editorializing, analysis, or judgment—just a summary of what was said. Then change roles. Afterward, take another two minutes each to comment on the process. Remember, the purpose is to state your observations, not push your point of view. This is not a time to settle or resolve disputes, only to hear one another. In the bargain, you may find you have a new understanding of the problem, which may help you solve it later.

Soak Cycle

Notice how you respond when someone gives you a compliment or says, "I love you." Do you react as if you were on a volleyball court and just received a hit from the opposing side, making every attempt to lob the ball right back to the sender? Your child says, "I love you," and you, without missing a beat, say "I love you, too." A coworker says, "I like your outfit," and you say, "You look great, too." Or, in a variation on this theme, you deflect the kindness. "Thanks for a wonderful dinner," your wife says, and you reply, "Oh, it was nothing." Did you really hear the compliment or the words of appreciation? Probably not. The words danced over your consciousness like rain off a duck's back.

Switch your mind to the soak cycle. When people say, "I love you" or pay you a compliment of any sort, don't decide whether you deserve it, what their true motives are, or whether they really mean it. Instead, inhale. Feel the warmth of the message. Soak the kind words in as though they were September sunshine, a loving massage, the scent of springtime. Exhale and say, "Thank you."

Good Advice

When a friend comes to you with a problem, do you immediately try to think of ways to solve it? Are you formulating nuggets of advice even as he or she speaks to you? When you give advice you usually leave the present moment behind. But when you listen, you enter the moment and allow yourself to respond with empathy and compassion. Just as you have a deep inner well of wisdom that you access more easily when you sink into the present moment, so too does your friend or loved one. Compassionate listening, not advice, is the best response to a friend in need.

What Are You Talking About?

There's an old story about a man who approaches a wise teacher to confess that he has spread gossip. Now, he says, he wishes he could take his words back. He asks the teacher how he can atone. The teacher says, "Take a feather pillow into a field, then open it up and release the feathers." The man does so and returns to the teacher. "Now," says the teacher, "there is one more thing you must do." The man says he is prepared to do whatever it takes. The teacher instructs, "Go and collect all the feathers."

Talking comes so naturally to us that we often don't pay attention to what we say and the power our words have. A conversation can take on a life all its own. Without consciously doing so, we may spread gossip, create rumors, and hurt other people's feelings and reputations. Our words cannot be taken back. They are like the feathers in the story. Like ripples in a pond, they set off waves far from where we stand. We rarely know how far they reach and what good or harm they ultimately accomplish.

Hear Yourself Talk

We know deep within us that words have power. The Bible tells us that God said, "Let there be light," and there was light. We say a man is as good as his word. Witches are said to cast spells with magical phrases. Notice the nature of your comments. Are you offering complaints, compliments, gossip, constructive commentary, idle conversation, pleasantries? What do you talk about? Do you believe what you say? Do you want to believe it? Do you project positive thoughts into the universe with your words or burden the atmosphere with negativity? Are these the words you want to release into the world? Try this: For every complaint you utter, try to say two good things. Treat your words as though they contain power and choose them carefully.

Give Up on Gossip

We like to believe that the stories we tell about other people are just trivial gossip. But gossip is rarely harmless. Just imagine yourself as a fly on the wall in someone else's kitchen listening to what is being said about you. Even seemingly innocuous conversation, when you are the subject and are discussed without your knowledge, feels invasive. Choose one day a week to be gossip-free. Mark it on your calendar.

Silent Partners

Sometimes the best way to gain awareness about a habit or behavior is to try to give it up. Try participating in an activity with your spouse or housemate in silence. Select a task that you will perform together without speaking. It may be gardening, cleaning the house, cooking a meal, or painting the kitchen. Observe how it feels to spend time with another person without words.

Emotional Terrain

Maybe one reason it is easier to maintain our mindful composure on—rather than off—the meditation cushion is that we are alone when we meditate. When we return to the world of cooperation, compromise, and competition, our serene state often dissolves. Through close relationships with others, our emotions, so-called "positive" and so-called "negative," have a tendency to flare up.

Notice what happens when you are overcome with emotion, be it anger, sadness, or joy. When you experience extreme states of emotion, your equanimity—your ability to detach from your thoughts and settle into the present moment in a clear and wakeful state—disappears. Observe yourself next time you fly into a righteous rage. Who or what is guiding your actions? Chances are you feel as though you've been swept into a tornado's path. It's important to gather information from your emotions without letting them carry you away.

Balancing Strong Emotions

Mindfulness practitioners often treat strong emotions as dangerous states that should be avoided at any cost. Anger is considered lethal, and many practitioners get the message that if they lead truly mindful lives they will never feel infuriated again. Anger is indeed a dangerous emotion — if it is allowed to dictate your speech and actions. Instead, regard anger as a messenger. Often the message it carries is that someone is stepping on your toes, literally or figuratively. Observe your anger, but don't follow it. Listen for the insight it contains, but don't let it be your voice. Try not to act until it passes. Simply state that you are feeling angry now and will gladly discuss the situation or problem once you calm down.

Feel Now, Act Later

In meditation practice we learn to observe thoughts and feelings. If our minds begin to follow any particular sensation, be it anger, pleasure, desire, or repulsion, we are instructed to gently return to our breath. In that moment when our focus changes, we may be aware of an inner sensation like a quiet "click." That's the moment when we've broken off from a train of thinking that could carry us away in a direction against our will.

Look for that click of detachment when you feel anger coming on. You may be unloading groceries with your teenager when she announces that she will no longer baby-sit for her younger brother. Notice the heat of anger rising inside you, but don't react to it. Watch it as if it were a fire burning on a distant horizon. After you feel the subtle click of detachment, ask yourself what information the anger was trying to convey. When you feel calmer, you can use that information during a levelheaded and productive conversation.

To Forgive, Divine

Forgiveness is one of the most misunderstood concepts in human relationships. To forgive does not mean to accept bad behavior. It doesn't mean that you weren't hurt or that the other person wasn't wrong. Forgiveness is like canceling a debt. You simply

104

wipe it off the books. When you forgive someone, you let go of your anger and resentment so you can find peace and move on. You let go of the suffering you feel every time you think of the person or situation in question. You are not letting someone else off the hook; you are letting yourself leave the past behind so you can move into the present moment.

Make a grudge list. Write the names of all the people you haven't forgiven and what their offenses were. For example, you may write *Alex, for lying to me*. Picture your anger as a dark cloud that is hovering above your head. Notice that you are holding a string in your hand that is attached to the cloud and keeps it in place. Feel your fingers wrapped tightly around the string. Now release the tension

> *"When we see men of a contrary character, we should turn inwards and examine ourselves."*
>
> — Confucius

you are holding in your hand. Watch your palm open. See the cloud, free now, blow away. Watch as it gets smaller and smaller, then disappears. If there are tears, let them come. You need not rush through your list, but keep working at it, one person or infraction at a time. You'll probably find you need to put yourself on that list, too. Forgiving yourself can be the most difficult of all.

Release the Past to Enter the Present

Acceptance is part of forgiveness. In order to forgive yourself you must see your past as a blessing, not as a burden. Look back through your life. Is there a decision you regret? A choice you are still punishing yourself for having made? Now is the time to release the past. You can't live in the present moment if you haven't let go of the past.

Count the Ways

Which emotional experiences do you focus on most? If you have an argument with your spouse do you replay it in your mind for days afterward? Do you rehash it with friends? Ask yourself if you spend as much energy and time magnifying the loving aspects of your relationships as you do the difficult ones. Elizabeth Barrett Browning wrote, "How do I love thee? Let me count the ways." Notice what you are counting in your life. Do you tally your grievances or your reasons for gratitude? Make a list of everything you love about the person with whom you are in conflict.

Meditate on Love

There is a special meditation that helps practitioners magnify the love in their hearts and then extend that love to people and animals near and far. It is called *metta* meditation (metta is a Pali word for lovingkindness). Sit quietly and focus on your breath. As you feel yourself sink into a relaxed, mindful state, search inside for a pure, joyful feeling. Keep your attention on that image or feeling. As you pay attention to joy, watch it grow. Feel it permeate your body like a soft, warm light. Bring your attention to love. When you find a pure nugget of love in your being, breathe into it and feel it expand. Feel it radiate through your entire body. With each breath, feel your lungs and heart fill with joy and love.

Now picture someone close to you and imagine transferring some of your joy and love to that person. Notice that you are not depleted of any of the joyful, loving feelings you have created. There is an unlimited supply. Picture this person filling with joy and love. Now extend these feelings to everyone in your family — your partner, your children, your parents. Keep extending the feelings to more and more people: your neighbors, the residents of your town, your state, and your nation. Imagine lovingkindness circling the globe. Give more and more joy and love away while still noticing that your own supply has not decreased at all. There is plenty to give. Extend these feelings as far into the universe as you can imagine. Silently wish for all people, animals, and beings to be filled with joy and love.

When a Friend Is in Need

When a loved one is in trouble, we too feel troubled. First, we worry. Then we formulate ideas about what should be done to fix the situation. But perhaps the best thing we can do for our loved one and ourselves is to humbly acknowledge that we don't know the best solution. Instead, meditate on a pure and caring thought about your loved one. Picture him surrounded by radiant light. See his best qualities as starbursts increasing the light that surrounds him. Allow your love and concern for him to merge with that growing cushion of light. Hold this good feeling in your heart every time you think of him and his dilemma.

Child's Play

Parenting presents great challenges—and opportunities—for mindful living. On one hand, children by their very nature demand your attention, seemingly deflecting it from yourself. Caring for children often requires dividing your focus in many directions and doing several tasks at once, which can easily unsettle your hard-won equilibrium. And yet children are instinctive teachers. Whether you  have children of your own or are an aunt, an uncle, or a neighbor to those of others, you can learn a lot with and from young people.

Proud Parents

Even before your children were born you likely had hopes and dreams for who they would become. Chances are they've turned out different than you expected. Maybe they've exceeded your hopes, or maybe they've fallen short in some way. Accepting your children for the unique people they are can be a challenge. In this moment, see each child exactly as he or she is. Let go of your hopes, fears, expectations, and disappointments. Look at your child without wanting to change—or preserve—anything about her. Now try to see beyond what your senses can observe. Look with your heart at your child's essence. See the core of joy, openness, hope, and wonder that he embodies.

The Children's Hour

Young children have no trouble at all living in the present moment. The scent of anything from laundry detergent to a freshly cut lemon may fascinate, disgust, or intrigue them. They reach out to touch a cat's fur, a lady's feather hat, a shiny necklace. They taste raindrops, hop into puddles, and roll in the snow before they learn to grouse about the weather. They are alive to their senses. They are curious about every treasure life offers. And they know how to live outside of time.

Every now and then, rather than insisting that your children grow up, let them remind you to loosen up. Choose one activity

110

each day that will run on "child time." This may be a meal, a bath, or a story. During that time, don't rush your children along; let them set the pace. Avoid saying, "Don't touch"; instead, try to feel what they do.

Erase Attention Deficit

There is a lot of talk these days about attention deficit disorders of various kinds in children. We blame the media and our fast-paced society for children's short attention span. But some of the blame lies closer to home. Children learn to rush from activity to activity by watching the adults around them. We are so keen on making sure our children can compete in school and in life that we try to make each moment productive.

Help your children learn to be still by encouraging day-dreaming and introspection. Try having silent car rides during which the radio is off and everyone thinks his or her own thoughts. When you reach your destination you can share what was on your minds. Don't criticize your children for "drifting off into la-la land." Along with asking your children what they did in school, ask what they thought about and how they felt, too.

Act Childish

Ever notice how when you take a toy away from a baby she cries ferociously, as though there could never again be another happy moment? And then, a moment later, she is cuddling with her blanket as if there were nothing but softness and contentment in the world? We would do well to let ourselves move effortlessly from emotion to emotion the way very young children do. Be sad when you're sad, but don't cling to the feeling. Let feelings pass as naturally as clouds slipping gracefully across the sky.

The Definition of Joy

Children so often embody the meaning of the word joy—just watch a child play in a swimming pool or scoop up a bouquet of wildflowers. Think of yourself as a child and recall what gave you joy when you were young. What did you love to do? Did you have a favorite hiding place? A tree you loved best of all? A special doll or stuffed animal? Reintroduce one of your favorite childhood objects or pastimes into your adult life and reconnect with the childlike joy that still lives inside you.

Perfect Angels

If only children were always the perfect angels they sometimes appear to be. The truth is, children argue, rebel, procrastinate, spill things, disobey, and throw tantrums (not to mention full plates of peas). And when they do, we are not always the angelic caretakers we wish ourselves to be. Keep in touch with your goals as a parent by having a ready phrase to bring you back to your center. A good one is, "I am a patient, loving, and kind parent." Another way to get instant perspective is to imagine your child grown and gone. With the eyes of premature nostalgia, the minia-ture king of the chaotic kitchen or the petulant teen with her fists on her hips looks, well, angelic.

Quality Time

You've heard it a million times: It's not the quantity of time you spend with your children, it's the quality. Make a commitment to spend time with each of your children—alone. This is a special time for just the two of you. Depending on the size of your fam-ily, you may choose to devote anywhere from a weekend once a year to an afternoon once a week with each child. Mark it on your calendar. Make this a date you never break.

Look at the Pictures

Next time your child asks you to read him a story, don't just recite the words and flip the pages. Let yourself get lost in the pictures the way he does. Notice the details the words don't mention. Imagine what happens next in the story rather than letting your mind wander off to what still needs to be done after you put him to bed.

Breathe Together

If you find it difficult to meditate because of the demands of parenthood, try to get your children in on the act. Put your baby or very small child in your lap while you center and relax. This may not be an experience of total stillness, but it can be a meaningful and rewarding time. Feel your child's rib cage move up and down as she breathes and try to match your breathing to hers. Give older children an egg timer and tell them that you are going to have quiet time until the timer goes off. Explain that you will keep your eyes

closed and look at the pictures in your mind without speaking. Invite them to do the same, and allow them to draw, look at pictures, or read if they get bored before the time is up. Start with short intervals of just a few minutes and try to increase the time you can sit together quietly.

Celebrate with Soul

Listen to what people say when a big holiday approaches. You will likely hear complaints about how commercial the holidays have become, how they have lost their meaning, or that they are just another day. But it's not the holiday that loses its meaning, it's we who lose touch with why it was put on the calendar in the first place. Perhaps the customary celebration no longer suits your needs. If so, why not alter the tradition to suit you rather than celebrate the holiday halfheartedly or do away with it altogether?

Happy Birthday

Birthdays offer the perfect opportunity to focus your attention on the progress you've made in your soul's journey. After all, the day of your birth is the day you made your entrance into the world as a conscious being. How have you grown in the past 12 months? Make yourself a birthday card. Throw yourself a party. Buy yourself a present that affirms your commitment to reaching your full potential. Celebrate your dedication to being not merely alive, but truly awake.

A Wonderful Year

On New Year's Eve, rather than making resolutions for the year to come—which you will most likely break, anyway—reflect mindfully on the year that just passed. Make a list of 101 wonderful things about the year gone by. It may seem difficult, but take your time. Look at your calendar or skim your journal for reminders. Add to your list over the course of a week. Think of events both big and small: The birth of a child and the sight of a blue jay perched on your windowsill each merits a place on your list. Don't overlook the everyday wonders in life. Record your improving relationship with your father-in-law, the cozy coffee shop you discovered just a block from your office, and the joy you felt when you opened the first letter your niece ever sent to you.

Wrap It Up

Giving gifts doesn't have to be a wholly material pursuit. Giving presents to others is a good time to reflect on and expand your love for the people in your life. Make gift wrapping a meditation. As you choose the paper, size it, fold it around the gift, and decorate the package with bows and ribbons, hold an image of the recipient in your mind. Meditate on the joy of giving your love and attention to that person.

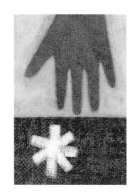

The Gift Is in the Present

The best present you can give for any holiday is the gift of being present. Instead of spending money on another tie, necklace, or sweater, make a gift certificate that offers the recipient a massage —not by a professional but with your own hands—or a quiet dinner for two, an hour of listening, or an evening together with no distractions (consider including the cost of a baby-sitter as part of the gift, if needed).

Cut It Out

It's hard to find the perfect card for someone you love. Even after visiting several stores, you still may not find a card with the right

118

message or image with which to communicate your true feelings. Instead, pull out several magazines and flip through the pages for pictures, words, and phrases that describe the recipient. This is an opportunity to really think about the person you are celebrating. Take time to appreciate all the aspects of the one you love and admire, and select pictures that represent as many of those facets as possible. Arrange and paste the images onto a blank card, then apply a layer of decoupage paste to give your collage a finished look.

The Life of the Party

Some people dread parties. The need to make small talk makes them feel awkward. Even the most outgoing people sometimes feel out of place in certain social situations. Next time you're at a gathering where you feel alone or disconnected, don't mope or retreat. Find someone who looks more ill at ease than you feel and ask him a few questions about himself. Or ask the hostess what you can do to lend a hand—perhaps clear the used dishes, load the dishwasher, or help serve the next course. In the process, you change your attitude from self-pity to service.

Mind Your Business

WHAT DO YOU DO?" This is often the first question we ask a new acquaintance. We define people by the work they perform. Work, in turn, has defined human experience since the beginning of time—or at least since Eve ate the apple and God announced that man would be bound to a lifetime of toil. And for just as long, it seems, men and women have endeavored to be free of work. Some sixteen hundred years ago, before "follow your bliss" was a common catch phrase, Saint Augustine, at age thirty-three, gave up his post as a rhetoric teacher to live a life of the mind. These days we accept a TGIF mentality, counting down the days until the weekend when we can leave the office behind.

As a culture, we seem to be of two minds about our need for work and our desire for leisure. Despite all of the laborsaving devices we have at our disposal, statistics show that we spend fewer days and hours enjoying time off than in the past. Even with the miracle of machines that answer our phones, clean our clothes, and wash our dishes, we are a nation deprived of rest. Instead of using technology to free up our time, we use laptop computers, cellular phones, pagers, and Internet access to keep us wired for work.

In the decades since the advent of the computer, Americans have worked more hours, not fewer, than the generation before. The idea of doing one thing at a time has been replaced by the need to multitask — to simultaneously conduct business over the phone, compose e-mails on the computer, and surf the Web for even more opportunities. Meanwhile, the time we have to reflect, to enjoy our families and friends, and to participate in community-building activities is slowly disappearing.

Studies show that overwork leads to increased stress and addictive behaviors, such as alcoholism. The cost to our soul has not been calculated, but we sense that the demands of our industrial and information economy are taking their toll. This state of affairs may never change as long as we believe that we must work more hours to earn more money to increase our assets. But wealth is not a pile of gold coins or a stellar stock portfolio. According to the *Oxford English Dictionary,* wealth is simply "the condition of being happy and prosperous; well-being."

"Let the beauty we love be what we do."

— Rumi, 13th-century poet and mystic

Eyes on the Prize

You may love your work; if so, you're lucky. But no matter what you do for a living, there's more to who you are than just a job title. Remember why you work. It may be to support your family or to pay for the time you spend scuba diving in the Caribbean. Maybe work is your way of doing service and helping others. No matter what your larger purpose is, find a way to remind yourself of it while you're on the job.

Choose a corner of your work space as a place to reflect your goals and aspirations. You could keep your paperclips in a pottery dish your daughter made at day camp to remind you of the family you are at work to support. Or you may design a mouse pad with a photograph of the mountain getaway you are saving to revisit. If there is a person who inspired you to take up your line of work, you could post his picture or a quote he used in a spot where you'll see it often throughout your workday. Rather than slipping into a mindset in which you value your job because

124

of the paycheck it produces, remember to make your vocation valuable by bringing your full awareness to the workplace.

Take Your Values to Work

"Take Your Child to Work Day" has become a popular event in offices across the nation. A trend worth starting is "Take Your Positive Values to Work Day." Often the values we associate with conscious living— behaving in a kind, loving, and patient manner—are left behind when we leave our house for work in the morning. While you're still at home, call your voice mailbox at work and leave a message that will help you start off on the right foot when you listen to it at your desk. Perhaps you'll want to remind yourself of a different value to focus on each day, such as cooperation, humility, or gratitude.

Inspiration Close at Hand

Keep a copy of an inspirational article or a book of inspirational quotes near your computer. Reach for it while you wait for files to download or programs to boot up.

Work Soft

We're encouraged to work hard, but never to work soft. Yet too much effort can be counterproductive. We may work too hard at the expense of our ability to think clearly, to be in touch with our intuition, or to operate in a relaxed and efficient manner. Each time the phone or fax machine rings, use it as a reminder to relax your shoulders and breathe deeply. Soften your focus as you sink back into your body.

126

Clear Work Clutter

Apply some principles of feng shui to your workstation. Take a good look at the items that are in your field of vision. Clear the clutter from your bulletin boards and desktop. Take down old pictures, cartoons, or anything else that no longer supports your sense of prosperity and well-being.

Bring Home to Work

These days, with the advent of cell phones and laptop computers, work doesn't necessarily end when you leave the office. More and more people now bring work home. Why not also bring your true home (your mindful state) to work? Anytime you find yourself waiting for a meeting, a printout, or a fax, drop into the present moment. Sit in your chair and become conscious of your breathing. Feel your feet touching the floor, your thighs resting on the seat. Make sure your back is supported and your shoulders are relaxed. Submerge as deeply into this moment as you can. Don't plan or think. Just be.

One Task at a Time

Multitasking is a reality of the modern workplace. The fact that there is now a word for the practice of doing several things at once shows that the conflict between doing and being is more powerful than ever. We check our e-mail while making a phone call, eat our lunch while reviewing reports, and talk to a coworker while sending a fax.

This contemporary juggling act can easily get out of hand. You can't necessarily stop multitasking altogether, but you can gradually scale back. Start by noticing how many tasks you are doing at a given moment. Ask yourself which one is the highest priority. Delete the activity that is lowest on the list. This may mean turning off a radio, putting down your coffee, or putting someone on hold. You'll be more effective at the one thing (or even the two) that you are still doing.

Think before You Click

Technology has upped the speed limit at work, but you still have the ability to apply the brakes. Identify the tasks that really demand high-speed technologies. For the rest, shift down a gear. Consider walking a memo to the office down the hall rather than e-mailing or faxing it. Mail a letter when e-mail isn't necessary. Sometimes the time it takes for a piece of mail to reach its destination is the time both the sender and the recipient need to sort out the facts or simply to rest between making one decision and taking action on another.

Take a Productivity Break

Studies have shown that workers who take short breaks every 45 minutes or so are more productive. That's because the conscious brain tends to stay focused and work best in 45- to 60-minute intervals. If you can program your computer to give you a signal every 45 minutes, do so. Get up and stretch your legs, get a drink of water, or step outside and walk across the parking lot and back. When you return to your desk your mind will feel refreshed.

A Little Shut-Eye

In the middle of a hectic workday even a 10-minute break can seem like an impossibility. Try this minimeditation when your break time gets edged out of your schedule. Close your eyes—just for the length of an inbreath and an outbreath if that is all the time you can take. This quick retreat from surrounding stimuli and stress can help you refocus your mind and gather your energy.

Quiet Your Mind

Carla Hannaford, Ph.D., a neurophysiologist, an educator, and the author of *Smart Moves,* offers some simple exercises to help the brain function better. Although she focuses her research on how to help children in the classroom, her techniques can benefit anyone. This technique, called "Hook Ups," calms the mind and improves concentration. In a standing or sitting position, cross your right ankle over your left one. Now cross your right wrist over the left. Turn your palms so they face one another, and link your fingers. Bend your elbows out and gently turn your fingers in toward your body until they rest on the breastbone in the center of your chest with your knuckles facing up. Let yourself relax into this position. Breathe evenly. Notice that you feel calmer than you did before you began. Hold this position for as long as you like.

Office Yoga

Here's a yoga pose you can practice at work that won't require a change of clothes or a special mat. In fact, you can do this pose any time you want to calm your mind. All you need is a chair without wheels. Stand a couple of feet from the back of a chair with your feet shoulder-width apart. Exhale and bend forward from the hips. Hold your elbows with your hands and rest your forearms across the top of the chair's back until you can place your forehead on your arms. Make sure that your feet are parallel and that your knees are relaxed and not locked. Feel your feet in contact with the floor and feel supported by the strength in your legs. Let your spine relax. Let the muscles in your face and neck relax, too. Breathe easily. When you are ready to straighten up again, feel your feet firmly rooted on the floor, then inhale and lift to an upright position from the strength in your legs.

A Little Work Music

Office sounds are not always conducive to relaxation. The clanking of automated folding machines, the whir of the copier, the intermittent ring of the fax machine, and the random chatter from other offices or cubicles can be distracting at best, irritating

at worst. Music, on the other hand, helps reduce stress levels, increases creativity and IQ levels, sharpens concentration, and improves all-around brain function. Studies have shown that subjects who listened to Mozart before taking a test had better scores.

The right background music can have positive effects. Choose music that inspires you but won't distract you, your coworkers, or your clients. Jazz and classical music are good options. If your workplace isn't conducive to using a sound system that your coworkers can hear, use headphones to listen to a portable CD player or the CD player on your computer.

Break Time

Companies allow time for workers to eat a midday meal. Use this time not only to eat, but also to nourish yourself in other ways. Find a quiet place to close your eyes and do focused breathing for 5 or 10 minutes before returning to your job. You can also take a break from your usual coffee break by drinking soothing chamomile tea instead. Rather than a cigarette break, take a short walk. Even a stroll around the parking lot will help you feel refreshed.

Get the Big Picture

The phone rings, you pick it up. On the other end, the caller is complaining about your company's products, service, or performance. Your mindful state evaporates. You feel your jaw clench, your shoulders go rigid, and your brow furrow. To respond in a conscious way, you need to shift your focus.

Look up from your desk, computer monitor, or phone and notice the bigger picture. Your world is not confined to the angry voice on the phone. The stress that has just spread its tendrils inside you is not the only reality. Stand up. Look around; take in the view of your entire office. The angry caller is now just one element in a broader context. Keep a globe or map of the constellations near your desk to remind you of an even larger perspective whenever a negative interaction threatens to take over your mindset. This way, you can keep conflicts confined to a smaller section of your mind, making room for clarity and control.

Make a Pie Chart

Pie charts and graphs are frequently used in the corporate world to illustrate various economic trends. Make a pie chart of your own, using these labels for each slice: Work, Recreation, Spirit/Reflection, Home/ Family, and Community/Friends. Let the size of each slice reflect the amount of time and mental energy you put into each

"Work consists of whatever a body is obliged to do ... play consists of whatever a body is not obliged to do."

— Mark Twain, *The Adventures of Tom Sawyer*

aspect of your life. Make a new chart each month. See whether the slices of your pie begin to even out as you focus your attention on balancing your life.

Give Your Screensaver Meaning

What's on your computer monitor at work? Is the screen you face day in and day out decorated with a pattern that appeals to you? Or is your screensaver set to some random geometric pattern or the logo of the company that manufactured your machine? Choose a monitor design and screensaver consciously. What would you like to look at each day? Some computers offer images of swimming fish, tropical beaches, or even the option of scanning in a photograph of your own. If you can program your computer to display a "scrolling marquee," a word or phrase that floats across your monitor after the computer has been at rest for a short time, key in a phrase that you really need to see.

Don't Call It Work

You can change your attitude by consciously choosing your words. Rather than saying you are going to work, which sounds like an unappealing obligation, say you are going "to the studio," "to teach," "to create," "to help," or "to build." Focus your word choice on the playful, imaginative, active, or positive aspect of what you do. See what a difference a word can make.

Early Retirement in Your Mind

It's easy to take your job, your coworkers, and even your supervisor for granted. But chances are there are some things you truly appreciate about your work life. Try this: Imagine today is your very last day of work. See yourself packing up your desk. Notice the details. You are putting your pictures, pens, coffee mugs, and

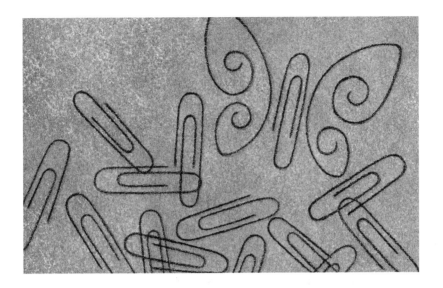

magnets into cartons. Your coworkers are stopping by your desk to say goodbye. See their faces. Listen to what they are saying. Are they telling you they'll miss you? Saying what a good job you've done? What are you thinking now? Which of them will you miss? What will you miss doing now that your employment is over? When you finish this meditation, return to work with a new awareness of the things you truly appreciate about your job.

Your Work Is Calling

Members of the clergy say God called them to their mission. The Buddhists speak of finding your "right livelihood"—a way to make a living that causes no harm, supports your values, and addresses an authentic need. Everyone has a divine purpose. Your calling, or your true work, is where your passion and the world's needs intersect. Make a list of things you love to do. Let yourself fantasize a job that incorporates that activity in a useful way. Listen carefully to see if you can hear what purpose is calling you.

Do What You Love

In ancient Greece the word *chiros* meant the state of mind a person enters when she loses track of time. You experience this when you engage in an activity you love, whether it's playing the guitar, taking a morning jog, or sewing a dress. If you find yourself in this state at work, you've likely found a job that incorporates your passion. If not, see if there's a way you can bring a *chiros-*

inducing activity to work. For example, if you enjoy working with your hands, offer to build a new set of shelves for your office. Perhaps you love to be around kids but are employed at an insurance company. Offer to organize the company picnic and plan activities for employees' children. If you love to write, volunteer yourself as the editor of the company newsletter.

What Do You Want to Be When You Grow Up?

Just because you're an adult doesn't mean you've figured out what you want to be when you grow up. One way to find out—or to remember—is to take a time machine back to your childhood. Did you love taking off on Saturdays with your dog and a pack filled with sandwiches to follow a neighborhood stream and pretend you were an ex-

> *"Tell me, what is it you plan to do with your one wild and precious life?"*
>
> — Mary Oliver, *The Summer Day*

plorer? Maybe as an adult you'd like to research job opportunities that involve travel. Were you the kind of kid who would take apart the living room clock, try to put it back together, and not even mind that it cost you your television privileges? You may want to find a job where you are responsible for problem solving.

139

Envision Your Dream Job

If the job you are in is not your ideal one, take a step toward getting there. Reality often begins with a dream. Picture your dream job in your mind's eye. Imagine where you would work. What would

the physical setting look like? Whom would you be working with? What would you be doing? See as many details as you can. Now look through magazines for images resembling that situation. Cut out pictures and paste together a collage of your dream career. Post the collage on the inside of your closet door so that you can look at it as you dress for your current job. Or put it inside your briefcase so that you can take a peek while you're at work.

Identify one step you can take toward getting there, such as brushing up your resume, making a list of companies where you could pursue that profession, or signing up for a night class to acquire a skill you'd need.

The Best You Can Be

Too often we think of work as a grown-up version of school. The boss takes the place of the nasty principal who punished us every time we tried to have fun. The woman who works at the next desk is like the girl who always got the cutest boyfriend and wouldn't let you forget it. Your annual review feels like report-card day, when someone else tells you whether you passed or failed.

Work doesn't have to be this way. Our real job, as adults, is to offer our strengths and talents to the community at large. Work is one arena for sharing these gifts. You probably took your current job because it requires some skill that you possess. It may call on your ability to write, to work with your hands, to interact with people, or to organize details. This may or may not be what you consider the best way to showcase your talents, but it is the way you have right now. Make it your workday mission to be the best you can at what you do, to polish and perfect your skills, and to share them with the world. Affirm, "I am good at the work I do, and the work I do does good."

Money Matters

Money gets a pretty bad rap in Western culture. Everyone seems to chase after it, but at the same time we've declared a moral war against it. Sure, we say, "Money makes the world go around," but we also say, "Money is the root of all evil," "The best things in life are free," and "Money can't buy happiness." This love-hate relationship with finances can be harmful to our mental state.

It is difficult to find a healthy balance between spending and saving, between living within our means and living comfortably. The love of money can pull us away from some of our core values, and greed can get in the way of our impulse toward generosity. Of all our basic needs—food, shelter, clothing—money is the only one that we truly could live without.

Prehistoric man survived without money and, theoretically at least, we still can. Without credit cards, ATMs, bills, and coins, there would still be trees and wood with which to build shelters, and plants would still bear fruit for us to eat. Money and trade are human inventions, although we tend to think of them as intrinsic to life itself.

We confuse the value of cash with the value of what it can buy. For example, we cannot eat a one-hundred-dollar bill, although we can eat what we buy with it. The actual piece of paper, notation on our bank account, or plastic card is, in itself, useless. It won't keep us warm, but the house we buy with it will. The money itself has no inherent value. And yet in the world we live in, it is absolutely essential. Because money brings up so many emotional and moral concerns, it is essential to carefully consider our relationship with it.

> *"The cost of a thing is the amount of what I will call life which is required to be exchanged for it."*
>
> — Henry David Thoreau, *Walden*

Measure Your True Wealth

Wealth is about well-being. Try measuring your wealth according to a scale that accounts for more than just your financial status. The word prosperity comes from the Latin root *prosperus,* meaning "according to hope" or "to proceed hopefully." Prosperity, then, is a state of mind, not a bank account balance. Define prosperity for yourself. Affirm that you are prosperous.

Replace Greed with Gratitude

There is a Buddhist teaching that instructs followers to take pity on people who have the most material assets. They have a lot, the teaching goes, because in their weakness and insecurity they believe they need material comforts to survive. The person with very little should be regarded with admiration. He or she is not beholden to the fickle flow of material wealth but instead depends on the riches of a spiritual life.

Greed wants us to believe otherwise. Greed tells us that we will die without another car, that if we give to someone else, we lose. It's no accident that greed is among the seven deadly sins. Greed can kill; it certainly can kill the heart and soul. There is nothing more lethal to our loving and giving natures than a clutching fist. In fact, studies show that generous people are generally happier than those who are stingy.

Letting go is the opposite of greed. It is a spiritual practice. Let yourself be giving, not greedy. Next time you think of what you want or feel you must have, first take a moment to be grateful for what you already have.

Be Present While You Pay

When you pay your monthly bills, notice what you are thinking. If you are silently grumbling about the cost of heating oil or your tax bill, turn your mind around. Think instead of the comfort of being warm while it was sleeting outside earlier in the month. Let yourself feel grateful for your beautiful home and all the services your town provides, such as clean water that flows effortlessly into your pipes so you can use it whenever you want.

Paying the bills is seldom a highlight in anyone's routine. But it could be. Once you begin to think of it as a ritual for blessing all that you have—and affirming that you are grateful and happy to have those things—it may begin to feel like a time of celebration. Light candles or incense; make a special dinner. Think of paying the bills as an opportunity for rejoicing.

Natural Abundance

When you feel constricted, as though there is not enough money, food, or good things to go around, meditate on the bounty of nature. Take a walk in a natural setting and become aware of nature's extravagance. There is not just one kind of tree, there are hundreds — birch, sugar maple, elm, apple, chestnut, oak, beech, hemlock, and the list goes on. Now try to list every kind of flower you can. Look at a book of insects and note the vast variety of flying and crawling creatures that live in nature. Visit an aquarium and marvel at the multitude of shapes, sizes, colors, and types of fish that exist. We are living in a world that provides on

an extravagant scale. You are part of this world. Be open to the spirit of excess all around you. Affirm that abundance is a natural state in nature as well as in your own life.

Watch Financial Worries Disappear

Notice the effects your thoughts have on any given moment. Next time you find yourself worrying about how you will make your car payment, notice what that state of mind does to your body. Where do you feel tension? Are you clenching your jaw? Now remove the thought. Feel your body relax. Feel your mind relax.

A thought can be changed. Although you may still need to take steps to improve your financial situation, you don't need to cling to the fear and stress that accompany the thought about your car payment. Fear and worry don't improve a situation. They cloud your thinking and make it more difficult to act in a calm and productive manner. Next time you feel fear, worry, or stress, remind yourself that these are just thoughts. You can let go of a thought. Instead of worrying about your bills, think creatively about how to restore yourself to financial health. Affirm that you can do it.

Detach Here

When paying bills, you have a built-in reminder to separate your mind from past regrets, future plans, and worries about scarcity. As you prepare your payment, notice that there is a perforated line on the bill that separates the customer copy from the stub you send to the credit card, phone, or electric company. It reads "Detach here." Go ahead—follow the instructions. Notice what you are thinking, and then detach from any negative thoughts or emotions.

Make Your PIN Work for You

Every time you go to the ATM or access your money over the Internet or through a telephone banking system, you need to punch in a code of some sort. People often base their PINs, or passwords, on their birthdays, addresses, or names of pets. Instead, choose letter and number combinations that help you keep focused on your inner goals. For example, your PIN could be LTN247 if you want to remember to Love Thy Neighbor 24 hours a day, 7 days a week.

Checkbook Checkup

Leaf through your most recent checkbook registers and credit card bills. What are you spending your money on? Are you using your money to truly support your values? Do you profess to be a person who doesn't value material possessions, yet have a department store bill that makes the national debt look manageable? If you say you care about the fate of the hungry, have you written a check to a charity that feeds the poor? Are there places where your spending habits and your habits of mind are in conflict with one another? Check in once a month and notice whether these two sets of habits are moving closer together.

Give It Away

In the Old Testament, farmers are instructed not to harvest their crops too thoroughly, so that hungry wanderers may take some of the grains and vegetables left behind. You can heed this advice by leaving some of your monthly harvest for those in need. Give away a bag of clothes to Goodwill or the Salvation Army. When you purchase gas or milk at the convenience store, leave a handful of change in the collection jar on the counter for the community playground. Spend an afternoon volunteering at a soup kitchen or in one of your city's schools. Find a way to give some of your riches — be they time, money, or skills — away.

Love and Money

You probably value love over cold, hard cash. But what do you think more about? Do you worry about your bank account balance or analyze your stock and retirement options more often than you think about the love in your life and how you'd like to increase it? There is nothing wrong with having an intelligent plan to manage your assets, but you need to keep a healthy balance — in more ways than one.

When you find yourself worrying about money problems or shortages, take a moment to reflect on the abundance of love in your life and how much the people you care about are worth to you. Make it a habit to think about love more frequently than you think about money.

Quitting Time

We are surrounded by timesaving machines and devices that are meant to do some of our work for us, such as dishwashers and washing machines. We have ride-on lawn mowers, vacuum cleaners, and cars (think of the time you save by not having to hitch up a horse and wagon to get to the grocery store). So where is all our leisure time? Now that we have the capacity for time off it seems we need to learn how to use it.

No Result

What do you do for the pure pleasure of it? What do you love to do that will never appear on your resume, boost your bank account, win you praise, or enhance your appearance? Such activities may include meditating, sketching or doodling, napping, listening to music, playing an instrument you aren't particularly good at, collecting seashells that you later toss back into the ocean, or singing along with the radio.

The list is different for everyone. An artist probably can't sketch without thinking of the painting it may inspire, but a banker likely can. Only you know whether you love to swim because of how the water feels running over your body or whether you do it to lose weight. Whatever is on your list, make sure to build those activities consciously into your life. They are opportunities for minivacations in your hectic week.

Create an Oasis

Sabbath is the Hebrew word for pause. Make an oasis in your week, a time and place to pause and refresh your soul. From Monday to Friday you focus on the material aspects of life—earning money, buying food and clothes, achieving your goals on the physical plane. Make sure you also take time off from planning, plotting, and progressing to just be.

Find a way to put your urge to achieve, gain, and obtain on pause for an hour, an afternoon, or a day. Perhaps you will set aside an afternoon each week to turn off the telephone, television, or computer. Or you may simply take a bliss break. Walk through a greenhouse, read a favorite poem, float on your back in the community swimming pool, make a snow angel like you did as a child, listen to music, paint pictures, or sit beside a babbling brook and listen to what it has to say. Do whatever makes you feel awake and alive.

Take the Day Off

A day off means different things to different people. What does it mean to you? It may be a day of no obligations and no plans.

It may be a time for taking long walks, reading, gardening, building a model car, or doing a jigsaw puzzle. You may even choose to schedule a day of silence or solitude. Or you may put aside some time to play that old trumpet you haven't touched since high school.

On the Road

IF HOME IS OUR BASE of comfort and protection, the road is our means to adventure and the unknown. Americans, with a national heritage based on the pioneer's free spirit, are a people on the go. In a single year, Americans are likely to travel more than 827 billion miles on the nation's roads, rails, and airways.

Most of the roads we travel are well marked and mapped. We seldom find ourselves on that country road Robert Frost describes in his famous poem, a place where we must decide between more- and less-traveled routes. But as Frost's poem makes clear, the road is as much a symbol as it is a reality. And while we may not tread a rural byway like the one the poet describes, we frequently find ourselves at the figurative crossroads he conjures.

We may, for example, be in the boss's office deciding whether to take a promotion or go back to school to study architecture. Or we may be sitting up late in bed with our spouse deciding whether it's time to have a child. Our road is our life. It is our path, the direction we choose.

Philosophers throughout the ages have equated living life with taking a journey. The Taoists speak of a universal flow and of following "the way." Asian arts, such as *karate-do, tae kwon do,* and *judo,* all end with the syllable *do,* which means "the way," or "the path." The code of laws in Judaism is called *Halakhah,* which translates as "the walking," or "the path."

These paths are not found on any map. In fact, it seems that it is only as we grow older that we can see where our life's journey has been leading. At times, when the road we travel seems full of metaphorical potholes, one-way streets, and speed traps, we may wish there were a clearly charted course. If only we could purchase a tidy map that folds on well-worn creases to help us plot the easiest way. But of course that is not how life works. After all, the journey — not the destination — is everything.

"There is no place to go and nothing to get."

— Zen saying

156

No Hurry

Wherever you are going, don't rush. You may need to move quickly to get to that meeting, doctor's appointment, or school play on time. But you needn't get into a frazzled, harried state. Just as the Zen philosophers say that pain is inevitable but suffering is not, so too may we say that speed is inevitable but rushing is not. In fact, the stress that a hurried state induces is apt to lead to mistakes (wrong turns, exceeding posted speed limits and consequently being detained by a state trooper) and therefore work against our goal of punctuality. A calm state of mind, even amid the storm of our self-imposed schedules, is essential for getting us where we're going safely and in a timely manner.

Travel a New Road

Break your routine. Take a new route to work, the grocery store, or any place you tend to travel on automatic pilot. Turn down a new street and notice your surroundings.

Parking Space Practice

Every time you park your car you have an opportunity to practice letting go. Let the first empty parking space you see go by. When you park one row farther back in the lot, leaving a nearer space empty, you are leaving a gift for the next person who comes along. You are also practicing the habit of giving rather than grasping.

Travel Down

We're used to seeing our lives as one long road that stretches from birth to death. Time is like a conveyor belt that moves us forward with military precision. But what if we were to see our lives and our journeys as having another dimension? Consider that this moment, this *now,* may not have a lot of real estate on the lateral plane but has a vast territory. It is like a rabbit hole that drops down. Let yourself drop into an eternal place that moves neither forward nor backward. Sinking down, touch the sparkling well of inner wisdom and peace, a place where your entire being connects with a sense of universal wholeness. As you travel through your days, move not only straight ahead, but also down and in.

Overdrive

Americans drive an average of 13,700 miles per year and spend 36 hours a year stuck in traffic. People spend so much time on the road that they have taken to installing in their cars television sets and VCRs, not to mention phones, highly sophisticated stereo systems, back massage pads, and computers. For many, a car is like a turtle's shell, a traveling home. Whether you commute long distances, use your car for recreation, or make shorter trips to ferry children to school and lessons, you can make the time you spend in your car more conscious by taking a few simple steps.

Start in Silence

Before you turn your engine off, turn off the lights, radio or CD player, fan, and air conditioner or heater. That way, when you start your car again, you'll start in stillness and silence. After turning on the ignition you can consciously choose, one at a time, what else you want to use. You may find that your mind needs a quiet interval between getting into gear and hearing the rock music you had on for your commute home last night, or that after a 10-hour stretch at the office, you're in the mood for classical music, not the news.

Put It in Park

When you get into your car, take a moment before you shift into drive to contemplate the trip you are about to make. Be conscious of the journey in front of you. Affirm your intention to drive safely and to travel with respect for the other people and animals who may cross your path. Inhale; exhale. Now start your engine. Do the same when you reach your destination. Before you leave the car, take a moment to feel grateful for the safe and easy trip you just took.

At first you may not feel as if you had a particularly easy trip. You may have hit traffic, taken a few wrong turns, or missed an exit. Put your travel experience in perspective. Think about how the same trip may have been a hundred years ago (a mere blink of the chronological eye). Most likely it would have been taken by foot or on horseback. If it had been cold or rainy, you'd now be

chilled or wet. If you'd been lucky enough to drive in a covered conveyance, you may have stayed dry, but the wheels of your wagon may have gotten stuck in the mud. A trip that just took you an hour may have taken the better part of a day.

In fact, if your commute to work is an hour's car ride, chances are you wouldn't have had that job several decades ago. You'd have worked closer to home, and your opportunities would have been fewer. The car you are now sitting in has opened many new possibilities for you. Breathe in gratitude for this miracle of modern transportation. Exhale and exit.

Radio Play

Listen to every song on the radio as if the "you" who is being sung to is your higher power or deeper self. The country top-10 station will suddenly become a treasure trove of philosophical insights. Ditto for the easy listening station. Try it with hard rock, too.

Be All Drivers

When driving down a busy highway, try this (open-eyed!) meditation. Notice the driver in the car next to you. Let yourself wonder where he is going. Is he wearing a suit? Maybe he's on his way to work. A sweatshirt? Perhaps he's heading to the gym. Imagine what he's hoping for right now: that his wife will forgive him for coming home late, that his daughter won't be waiting too long at her soccer practice by the time he arrives to pick her up.

Now look at the driver in front of that car. What is she thinking, hoping, or fearing? And the driver in front of her? There are more cars coming in the opposite direction. There are cars far in front that you can't see and cars trailing far behind you as well. This parade of people stretches all across the city, the state, and the country. Begin to realize that each car is the vehicle for another person and his or her hopes, fears, desires, loves, and longings. Each individual has his or her own life path, and each one is as important as your own. Feel yourself as one traveler among many. Feel yourself in this life, on this road, both singly and as part of a great cosmic caravan. Look again at all the people with whom you are traveling. Wish them all well (yes, even the woman who just cut in front of you). Wish them all peace and fulfillment.

Come to a Complete Stop

When you approach a stop sign, tune in to your internal chatter. Come to a complete stop and take a breath. Notice what you are thinking about. Is it positive or negative? Does it confirm the beliefs you want to uphold? Are you living in the past, present, or future? Take this opportunity to regroup and refresh your mind.

Waiting Game

We think of travel as movement, but in fact, a lot of travel time is spent standing still. We wait for buses, planes, trains, and stop lights. We wait in traffic, we wait in airports, and we wait in wait-ing rooms for the person we were rushing to meet! So often seen as a stumbling block, waiting can instead be an opportunity to focus on a mindful life.

Whenever you find yourself waiting, use the time to drop into the present moment. First, become aware of your breath. Just breathe and be conscious of the flow of air moving in and out of your lungs. Next, become aware of your body. Begin with the places where your body touches another surface, such as the seat, the gas pedal in your car, or the ground. Notice the places where your skin makes contact with your clothing. Just observe the various sensations. Then shift your attention to the places where your skin is exposed to the air. Again, just notice and be present.

164

Once you feel fully present in your body, become aware of the world around you. Don't judge, just notice. Hear the sounds around you. Listen for the quietest one. Become aware of smells, then sights. Notice colors, shadows, sunlight. If you are sipping a beverage, fully absorb the flavor. You may still be waiting to get to your destination, but in a sense, you have already arrived — in the present moment.

Notice the Space Between

In meditation we watch for the spaces between inbreaths and outbreaths and the intervals between thoughts. Waiting is simply the pause between one action and the next. It is the negative, or empty, space in our days. The Japanese have a word for the empty space in a piece of artwork: *yohaku. Yohaku* is considered as important as the areas where inked lines and shades of color create what we are used to regarding as the painting itself. Notice the empty spaces in your day, the spaces between what we have come to regard as the "purpose" of life. Begin to see the beauty and necessity of these intervals and appreciate their role in creating the exquisite pattern that is your life.

Life in the Slow Lane

Sometimes the hardest part about being held back or slowed down is the feeling of losing control. We want to direct the forward momentum of our lives, but we're hampered by a flight delay, a road construction project, or a car in front driving five miles below the speed limit. You can't necessarily control the world around you, but you can always be in charge of what's on your mind at any given moment. Keep a poem or prayer you want to commit to memory in your wallet, glove compartment, or pocket. Use this time to learn a few lines. Or, if you've already memorized a prayer or poem, take this time to meditate on it, line by line. You can even repeat a mantra or inspirational word or phrase. Focus your thoughts and your breath. You may find you're disappointed when you begin to move again.

Wait like the Mountains

A mountain is not impatient. A mountain does not mind waiting. When you find yourself waiting in line, take a lesson from the mountains. In yoga, the Mountain Pose helps the body learn

166

from the strength of the earth. Try this simple pose any time you are standing around. Position your feet hip-width apart. Let your arms relax at your sides. Feel your weight balanced evenly on both feet and on the heels and balls of your feet. Extend your toes to their full length. Check that your knees are relaxed, not locked, and use your thigh muscles to keep your

kneecaps lifted. Make sure your pelvis is not locked or tense and that your tailbone is tucked in, which keeps your lower back from overarching. Feel the vertebrae that make up your spine resting comfortably and effortlessly, one on top of the other. Use the strength of your abdomen to support your lower spine. Let your shoulders and neck relax. Make sure you are not tensing your jaw, tongue, forehead, or eyes. As you continue to stand, keep bringing your attention back to your feet, which are the stable base for this posture, and be aware of your body from the soles of your feet to the crown of your head while you remain standing still and quiet.

The People You Meet

As you travel from place to place, hire each person you meet to be your teacher. Go through the day assuming everyone has something to teach you. Watch how this attitude transforms your interaction with the lackadaisical checkout clerk at the grocery store from an experience in frustration to an exercise in patience.

Attention, Please!

In airports and bus and train terminals, you are likely to hear an important reminder. Blaring from the public address system or conductor's booth is the very word you need to hear: *attention*. You may hear, "Attention all passengers boarding flight 123" or "Attention all shoppers." Whenever you hear the word *attention*, know that this is a message for you. Heed the command. Pay attention—to your breath, to the present moment, to the thoughts that are parading through your mind.

Mind Your Manners

Travel brings you into contact not only with new places but also with new people. Manners have evolved to make those interactions more pleasant, as well as more meaningful. But etiquette has gotten a bad rap in recent years. Some behaviors that were once thought considerate are now looked on as old fashioned. Many acts of respect that were relegated by gender, such as a man holding a door open for a woman, are now considered out of date. In too many cases, though, the helping behaviors were discarded rather than the gender-role expectations that accompanied them. Manners are outdated or old fashioned only if we are no longer conscious of what they mean. Reexamine polite behaviors and invest them with true significance.

Thank You, Thank You

Prayer is a way to communicate on a spiritual level. The simplest prayer is easy to memorize: It is thank you. Try to say it, silently or out loud, one hundred times a day. Each time you see something beautiful, experience joy, or avoid danger, say thank you. It doesn't really matter to whom you direct this simple prayer, be it another person, God, or the universe at large. Each time you say it, truly feel grateful.

After You

When you hold the door open for someone (male or female), think about your desire to make his or her passage through the doorway, and through life in general, easier. When you let someone go ahead of you in traffic or in line, remember the importance of letting go of your own plans and schedules. When you say "please," really honor the effort another person is about to make on your behalf. Feel a genuine and healthy dose of humility.

Vacation Time

When you take time off from your workday routine, you need not take time off from your mindfulness practice. In some ways, it is easier to stay in the present moment while on vacation. After all, your activities are pleasant and usually of your own choosing. But it can also be difficult to resist rigid itineraries or to eschew the habits of planning and judging. Whether you are traveling to a far-off locale or taking a day-trip close to home, you can find many opportunities to heighten your awareness and proceed consciously.

Opt Out of the Next Photo-Op

Next family vacation, leave the camera at home. Sure, family photo albums and videotapes provide a treasure trove for later reminiscences, but too often we sacrifice the present moment for the impulse to record it for posterity. Also, having a camera can make us lazy. We count on the mechanical eye to see the scenery,

and we depend on the photographic process to take the place of memory. Instead, trust your mind to preserve what you want to remember.

An alternative way to create vacation memories and strengthen a different sense is to bring a portable tape player and make a cassette tape of sounds from your trip. You can record interviews with family members, traveling companions, and people you meet. You can tape the crashing ocean waves, birdsongs, a splashing fountain, the bustle at a charming café, and the sound of street musicians.

You may also want to bring a blank notebook instead of a camera. Use it to take turns recording observations about each day's events. Sketch—rather than photograph—your favorite scenes. Bring along a gluestick and scissors and paste ticket stubs and colorful cutouts from tourist maps and brochures onto the pages.

172

Travel at Home

Ever notice how traveling to another country heightens your senses? You notice everything. The blue bottle of water at a Parisian café charms you. You take the time to appreciate the beauty of a dewdrop on a bright pink bougainvillea blossom that has fallen onto your hotel terrace, or you are entranced by birdcalls you'd never stop to listen to at home. Everything seems

> *"Be rather the Mungo Park, the Lewis and Clark and Frobisher, of your own streams and oceans; explore your own higher latitudes."*
>
> — Henry David Thoreau, *Walden*

enchanting. Adopt this mindset at home. Notice the small things as if you've never seen them before. At the end of the day make a list of the remarkable common objects in your world.

Go Where Art Takes You

Artists create while in a heightened state of awareness, and when we view art we are often lifted to that plane. Visit a museum and let yourself be absorbed in a painting that captivates you. Sit or stand in front of it and truly try to see it. Let go of your judgments and analytical thoughts. Let your heart do the looking.

Wish You Were Here

Most vacationers consider a visit to the gift shop to purchase postcards an essential part of their itinerary. The postcard may picture a beach, castle, or prairie vista. On the back we pen a short message that can often be summed up by the popular postcard phrase "Having a great time, wish you were here." What if we applied this phrase to ourselves? How often, whether on vacation or at home, do we find ourselves doing something we know we enjoy but are not truly present to appreciate? What if we tell ourselves, "Hey, I'd be having a great time, if only I were truly here"?

Go to a shop that sells postcards or make your own. You can find blank postcards in many art supply and stationery stores. Decorate the front with watercolors, colored pencils, or collaged pictures from magazines. Choose or create a scene that reflects some aspect of your daily life. Write yourself a note on the back of the card, such as "Be here," "Breathe," or "Enjoy." Address it to yourself and put it in the mail. In a few days when you open your mailbox, you will have a wonderful reminder to be present — whether you are on vacation, at home, or at work.

It's Only Natural

When we visualize a calm, soothing environment, it's often a place in nature. Whether it's a beach, a mountain path, an outcropping of rock that protects us from the wind while we bask in the sun's warmth, a peaceful lake, or a babbling brook, most of us have a real or imagined natural haven. Nature is where we feel our connection to the elements. The beating heart seems soothed by the breath of the wind. Whatever its magic, nature nurtures the soul in a way that is deep, reliable, and nearly always accessible.

A good way to meditate outdoors is to keep a nature journal. All you need is a pencil and a blank book or a pad of paper. Spend a half hour looking at one flower or tree. Try to represent it on paper. You don't have to be an artist, and the final product is not the point. Don't cross out "mistakes." There are no mistakes. Start again or just keep going. No one else need see your drawing. In fact, don't even call it a drawing; call it a record of your ability to see. The point is to focus on every detail of shape, color, shade, and line. Before you know it, you'll be thoroughly absorbed in the task at hand and in the object you are rendering.

Look to the Stars

Ancient people saw the heavenly bodies as great reservoirs of energy. Taoists consider the Big Dipper a vital constellation and believe that the glittering ladle above our heads is an actual cup bearing cosmic energy. Find a place that is dark enough to show off the stars. Lie on your back and look up at the Big Dipper. Meditate on the energy it's believed to hold; imagine drinking from its bowl. Feel the light course through you, down your throat and through your heart and lungs until it settles in your lower abdomen. Let the stars' bright constancy fill your body.

A Stone's Throw

Go to a river, ocean, or any body of moving water. Walk along the shore and collect a handful of rocks. Think of habits of mind, fears, resentments, and outdated beliefs that you are ready to let go of. Feel the weight of a stone in your hand. Cradle the weight of the resentment or fear that has been stuck in your mind. When you are

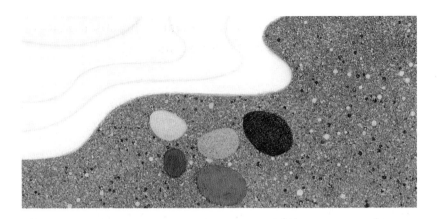

ready, toss the rock away, letting it carry with it your inner block. Watch as the water rushes over the spot where your rock fell into the water, making it disappear.

Timeless Moments

A moment is not a measure of time the way a second or a minute is. A moment experienced in its fullness exists beyond time. Find opportunities to live apart from the ticking of a clock. Try to tell time by the position of the sun. Make it a goal to come home from your vacation *without* a tan line where your watchstrap should be.

A Final Re-minder

RELIGIOUS PEOPLE SPEAK of making life holy. Living mind-fully means living life more wholly. In many ways, these approaches are the same. We bless ourselves, the people in our lives, and the environment around us when we pay them deep attention.

When our vision is not clouded by past regrets and future worries, we see the world like a nearsighted person who puts on glasses for the first time. Once-blurred lines come into focus. Colors appear more vibrant. Textures call out to be touched. When we live life consciously, our hearts open. As we feel moved to stop and listen to a sparrow sing, we also learn to listen more closely to our inner voice or intuition. Time does not so much fly by as settle down.

As you practice living mindfully, keep a journal of your experiences and take note of the changes you see in your life. At least once a year, look for opportunities to spend a weekend or a week developing your mindfulness practice. You may want to go on a meditation retreat, schedule a day of solitude at the seashore, or sign up for a workshop on mindfulness. These yearly tune-ups help you stay committed to 12 more months of the process—one moment at a time.

"The greatest discovery of our generation is that people can alter their lives by altering their attitudes of mind."

— William James

Index